Christianity and the Secular

Blessed Pope John XXIII Lecture Series in Theology and Culture

CHRISTIANITY
and the SECULAR

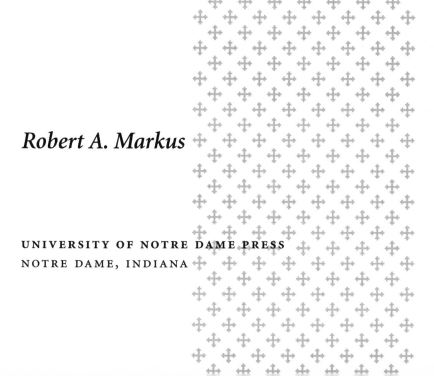

Robert A. Markus

UNIVERSITY OF NOTRE DAME PRESS
NOTRE DAME, INDIANA

Library of Congress Cataloging in-Publication Data
Markus, R. A. (Robert Austin), 1924–
Christianity and the secular / Robert A. Markus.
p.   cm. — (Blessed Pope John XXII lecture series in theology and culture)
Includes index.
ISBN-13: 978-0-268-03490-0 (cloth : alk. paper)
ISBN-10: 0-268-03490-7 (cloth : alk. paper)
ISBN-13: 978-0-268-03491-7 (pbk. : alk. paper)
ISBN-10: 0-268-03491-5 (pbk. : alk. paper)
1. Christianity and culture—History.   I. Title.   II. Series.
BR115.C8M2396   2006
261.09—dc22

                                        2005034404

One of the great satisfactions of my family's involvement in this series is rediscovering the great thinkers of the past, in this case, St. Augustine of Hippo. Equally rewarding is that this book, the first in the series, reminds me of a reality often ignored: the big issues of the past are often identical to the big issues of today. Robert A. Markus's short book takes on a large issue, arguably the root discussion of our times—the relationship of the sacred or religious to the secular. It is reassuring, in this world of turmoil and tensions between sacred and secular, to learn that Christianity, and St. Augustine in particular, encouraged a concept of "the secular," roughly equivalent to the common interests that can be shared by all who live in a society that is not religiously homogeneous.

Professor Markus points out that "the sacred and the profane were both familiar in antiquity; but until it was imported by Christianity, there was no notion of the 'secular' in the ancient world." If we understand the sacred as "roughly coextensive with the sphere of Christian religious belief, practises, institutions, and cult," then the profane "will be close to what has to be rejected in the surrounding culture, practises, institutions." But, as Markus points out, the secular "does not have such connotations of radical opposition to the sacred; it is more neutral, capable of being accepted or adapted. . . . It will be the shared overlap between insider and outsider groups, the sphere in which they can have a common interest and which—from the Christian point of view—need not be repudiated or excluded." Augustine, Markus argues, wanted to establish and vindicate a sphere—that of the civil community—in which both "secular" and "Christian" have a stake: not a third city between the earthly and heavenly, but their mixed, "inextricably intertwined" state in this temporal life. As he says, for Augustine, political discourse and institutions are concerned not with the ultimate realities of human fulfillment and salvation but with what, in Dietrich Bonhoeffer's language, may be called the penultimate things.

The author pays tribute to Blessed Pope John XXIII, whose vision liberated Catholics from a "cultural ghetto" and "amounted to an acknowledgement of the secular as an autonomous realm." It is an ideal whose decay Joseph Cardinal Ratzinger, soon to be Pope Benedict XVI, perhaps lamented when he declared, "Secularism no longer has that element of neutrality that opens up spaces of freedom for all." Robert Markus places this achievement in a Christian tradition reaching back at least to St. Augustine of Hippo. As Markus says, these questions that exercised Augustine are the fundamental questions of human social existence, and Augustine has something to say to us, no less than his contemporaries.

—Robert L. Dilenschneider

CONTENTS

ABBREVIATIONS AND SOURCES

AA: Auctores Antiquissimi
CC: Corpus Christianorum, Series Latina
CSEL: Corpus Scriptorum Ecclesiasticorum Latinorum
MGH: Monumenta Germaniae Historica
PL: Patrologia Latina
PLS: Patrologiae Latinae Supplementum

Ancient Sources Referred to in the Text

Auc. Hav. ext.: *Auctarii Havniensis extrema,* ed. Theodor Mommsen
(MGH AA 9 [*Chronica minora* 1], 299–339).

Augustine
De bono con.: *De bono coniugali* (*CSEL* 41)
De civ. Dei: *De civitate Dei* (*CC* 47–48)
De Gen. ad litt.: *De Genesi ad litteram* (*CSEL* 28)
De mor. eccl.: *De moribus ecclesiae catholicae et de moribus Manichaeorum*
     (*CSEL* 90)
Enarr. in Ps.: *Enarrationes in Psalmos* (*CC* 38–40)
De cons. ev.: *De consensu evangelistarum* (*CSEL* 43)
Sermo: *Sermones* (*PL* 38–39; *PLS* 2; *CC* 41)

C. Faust.: Contra Faustum Manichaeum (*CSEL* 25)
De vera rel.: De vera religione (*CC* 32)
De doctr. Christ.: De doctrina Christiana (*CC* 32)
Ep.: Epistolae (*CSEL* 34, 44, 57, 58, 88)

Boethius
In cat. Arist.: In categorias Aristotelis (*PL* 64)

Cassiodorus
De orth.: De orthographia (*PL* 70)
Var.: Variae (*CC* 96)
Exp. Psalm.: Expositio Psalmorum (*CC* 97–98)
Inst.: Institutiones, ed. R. A. B. Mynors (Oxford, 1937, 1961)
De an.: De anima (*CC* 96)

Facundus of Hermiane
Pro def.: Pro defensione trium capitulorum (*CC* 90A)

Gregory
Ep.: Epistolae (*CC* 140, 140A)
Hom. in Ev.: Homiliae in Evangelia (*CC* 141)
Hom. in Hiez.: Homiliae in Hiezechielem (*CC* 142)
Mor.: Moralia (*CC* 143, 143A, 143B)

Minucius Felix
Oct.: Octavius (*CSEL* 2)

Orosius
Adv. pag.: Adversum paganos (*CSEL* 5)

Otto of Freising
Chron.: Chronicon (*MGH*, Scriptores Rerum Germanicarum in Usum Scholarum, 1912)

Procopius
GW: Gothic War (Loeb ed., *Wars*, vols. 2–5)

Salvian
Ad eccl.: Ad ecclesiam (*CSEL* 8)

Tertullian
Apol.: Apologeticum (*CC* 1)

Vigilius
Ep. ad Rust. Seb.: Epistola ad Rusticum et Sebastianum (*PL* 69)

Other
CTh: Codex Theodosianus, ed. T. Mommsen and P. Meyer (Berlin, 1905)
CJ: Codex Iustinianaeus, ed. P. Krueger (Berlin, 1929)

INTRODUCTION

Lecturing in Cambridge six months before the outbreak of the last war, T. S. Eliot asked the question: Have we—he was, of course, thinking mainly of Britain—reached the point 'at which practising Christians must be recognised as a minority . . . in a society which has ceased to be Christian'?[1] He was not the first to raise the question; and it has been asked and answered, in one way or another, a thousand times since. While I was writing the lectures that constitute this book, the changing horizons of the discussion concerning secularisation were at the back of my mind—though quite a long way back. This is not what I shall discuss, but it lies behind much of what I have to say. I therefore begin with some brief remarks on this subject.[2]

The years following the war were, of course, a watershed—perhaps in Europe more than in America—in our habits of thought and speech as well as in many other ways. A great deal of earlier discourse on this theme, especially before the middle of the last century, now seems fatally dated. The very terms in which writers of the generation of T. S. Eliot, Jacques Maritain, and the Niebuhrs, to mention only a few, discussed the nature and ideals of

1. T. S. Eliot, *The Idea of a Christian Society* (London, 1939), 12–13. The lectures, published in October, had been delivered in March 1939.
2. For a recent survey (though with only slight coverage of theology), see P. Pasture, 'Christendom and the Legacy of the Sixties: Between the Secular City and the Age of Aquarius', *Revue d'Histoire Ecclésiastique* 99 (2004): 82–117.

their societies and their cultures now seem mainly of historical interest.[3] But questions concerning the 'secular' have not gone away. Relations between religion and public life have developed in very different ways on the opposite sides of the Atlantic, and even within Western Europe. Nevertheless, as the sociologists committed to what has been labelled 'the secularisation thesis' in the 1960s insisted, secularisation had its impact in America no less than in Europe. One of the best known of them, Bryan Wilson, noted that 'superficially, . . . and in contrast to the evidence from Europe, and particularly from Protestant Europe, the United States manifests a high degree of religious activity. And yet, on this evidence, no one is prepared to suggest that America is anything other than a secularised country.'[4] I quote this testimony simply to underline that despite appearances to the contrary, a general shift in horizons commonly referred to as 'secularisation' is accepted as a fact—or was, as we shall see, until very recently—on both sides of the Atlantic. Despite the great divide of the Atlantic, by the late 1950s and 1960s Christians on both sides of it began to feel obliged to come to terms with something they interpreted as secularisation, and many theologians to reinterpret Christianity in secular terms. The emphasis on the 'adulthood' of the world in Dietrich Bonhoeffer's late works, especially the *Letters and Papers from Prison*, first published in English translation in 1953, gave wide currency to theological attempts to construct a 'secular theology' or 'religionless Christianity' and to portray secularisation as representing a crucial strand in Christianity itself.[5] And, perhaps inevitably, historians of Christian thought were not slow to find warrant for such ways of thinking in Christian tradition.

3. For a particularly good discussion of secularisation that provides not only a historical account of this concept but also a constructive explication, see Robert Song, *Christianity and Liberal Society* (Oxford, 1997). On Niebuhr, see Stanley Hauerwas, 'The Liberalism of Reinhold Niebuhr', in *With the Grain of the Universe: The Church's Witness and Natural Theology* (London, 2001), 87–111.

4. Bryan R. Wilson, *Religion in Secular Society: A Sociological Comment* (London, 1966), 89.

5. See, e.g., his letters of 8 and 30 June and 16 and 18 July 1944 in Dietrich Bonhoeffer, *Letters and Papers from Prison*, ed. Eberhard Bethge, trans. Reginald H. Fuller (London, 1953), and *Ethics*, ed. Eberhard Bethge, trans. Neville Horton Smith (London, 1955), 62–63. It is thought unlikely, however, that Bonhoeffer himself would have been in sympathy with this development; I have not been able to consult Eberhard Bethge, *Die mündige Welt* (Munich, 1955–56).

This was the intellectual climate in which I wrote my book *Saeculum*,[6] and it would be dishonest to pretend that I was immune to its influence. It may have shaped, more than I intended, my attempt to understand what Augustine might have to say to Western Christians in the second half of the twentieth century. I was then inclined to see Augustine as one of the founding fathers of a Christian tradition of 'secularity'.[7] Was my approach to Augustine unduly swayed by the intellectual climate in favour of secularisation, was I simply swimming with the tide of intellectual fashion? This is one of the questions I have put to myself and shall try to answer in this book.

The fashion proved, in the event, to be rather short-lived. For as one of the gurus of 'secularisation theory', Peter Berger, wrote in 1999—only some thirty or forty years after the height of the vogue for secularisation— 'a whole body of literature by historians and social scientists loosely labelled "secularization theory" is essentially mistaken.'[8] The process of modernisation had been taken as the main motive force of secularisation in modern societies, especially in the industrialised world. But modernisation has gone on; secularisation, we are now told, has been reversed. Writing at the very end of the twentieth century, this former champion of 'secularisation theory' had come to recognise—along with a great many others—that modernisation could have quite the opposite effect. 'To say the least', he wrote, 'the relation between religion and modernity is rather complicated.'[9]

We may leave sorting out the complexity of that relation to the sociologists. All we need to note for our purpose is that the reverse, what some have called 'desecularisation',[10] has become a more recent preoccupation of

6. Robert A. Markus, *Saeculum: History and Society in the Theology of Saint Augustine* (Cambridge, 1970; 2nd ed., 1988). All citations are to the second edition.

7. In Markus, *Saeculum*. Here (172–73) I brought the (at the time widely popular) book by Harvey Cox, *The Secular City: Secularization and Urbanization in Theological Perspective* (London, 1965), into relation with this tradition.

8. Peter L. Berger, 'The Desecularization of the World: A Global Overview', in *The Desecularization of the World: Resurgent Religion and World Politics*, ed. Peter L. Berger (Grand Rapids, MI, 1999), 2. The paper, originally published in *National Interest* (1996/97), has also appeared in *Islam and Secularism in the Middle East*, ed. Azzam Tamimi and John L. Esposito (London, 2000).

9. Berger, 'Desecularization of the World', 3.

10. Notably the contributors to Berger, *Desecularization of the World*. I had used the same term to describe what I thought had happened in the culture of late Roman Christianity in Robert A. Markus, *The End of Ancient Christianity* (Cambridge, 1990), esp. 1–17 and 213–28.

sociologists of religion—and not only of sociologists. In a more apocalyptic version, Samuel Huntington has, famously, proposed that our world, to borrow George Weigel's expression, is becoming increasingly 'un-secularised' and drifting towards confrontations in which religious conflict is taking an ever-growing part.[11] While the rest of the world is, in Peter Berger's words, 'as furiously religious as ever', this time Western Europe is the exception that proves the rule: it 'bucks the trend [towards increasing religious resurgence]'.[12]

I have started with these shifts in sociological fashion to provide a backdrop to my discussion of the secular; but I have neither the inclination nor the ability to describe the social, religious, or cultural developments of our time. I do not propose in this book to take sides, or even to discuss these modern issues, several of them highly controversial, of secularisation or its contrary. My aim will be only to contribute to an understanding of the place occupied by the secular in Christian history and within a Christian understanding of society. I shall try to do so through exploring the origins of the notion and the place it held in Christian history until its eclipse in the course of the Western European Middle Ages.

I cannot dodge the task of giving some preliminary clarification of what I mean by the 'secular'. This has been no easy task, for the multiplicity of definitions on offer are all related to their contexts, and those are many. I shall be concerned with a cluster of ideas of which the secular is a part: the 'profane', the 'sacred', and the 'secular'. The sacred and the profane were both familiar in antiquity; but until it was imported by Christianity, there was no notion of the 'secular' in the ancient world. The word and the concept are both alien to Greco-Roman religion. It was relatively easy to distinguish the 'sacred' from the 'profane'; but the language of neither law nor religion offered a ready-made terminology for a third realm, the secular. (This state

11. Samuel Huntington, *The Clash of Civilizations and the Remaking of World Order* (New York, 1996), 96–101. For a critical view, see Fred Halliday, *Islam and the Myth of Confrontation: Religion and Politics in the Middle East* (London, 1996).

12. Grace Davie, 'Europe: The Exception That Proves the Rule?' in Berger, *Desecularization of the World*. Davie's essay contains a particularly lucid account of the issues involved in the debate over secularisation. Invoking a definition given by José Casanova, she concludes with him that 'the differentiation and emancipation of the secular spheres from religious institutions and norms remains a general modern structural trend' (78). On the corresponding process in Islam and the Arab world, see Tamimi and Esposito, *Islam and Secularism*.

of affairs is still preserved in romance languages. Modern French, for instance, lacks a term for 'the secular'. 'Le profane', often used as its equivalent, preempts the distinction allowed for in English usage between what can be labelled, respectively, as 'secular' and as 'profane', and *laïcité* has a narrower range of reference.[13] The cluster of problems associated with the secular and secularisation has, however, received plenty of attention—French sociologists of religion have spoken of 'sécularisation' just as have their anglophone colleagues.)[14]

In Greco-Roman antiquity, the sacred was what belonged to the gods and to their cults. The profane, in line with the etymology of the word, was what lay outside the sanctuary, around the shrine: the sphere of ordinary everyday life. In the course of the confrontation of pagan and Christian in the fourth century the word tended to become part of the language of exclusion on both sides.[15] In modern English it has kept its negative sense of ritual uncleanness, pollution, impiety, or blasphemous contempt for the sacred—in short, of some mark of exclusion from the sacred. Sacred and profane in this usage are contraries, mutually hostile spheres.

Let me suggest that we keep 'sacred' and 'profane' as mutually exclusive areas. From a Christian point of view the 'sacred' will be roughly coextensive with the sphere of Christian religious belief, practises, institutions, and cult. 'Profane' will be close to what has to be rejected in the surrounding culture, practises, institutions—perhaps more or less identifiable with what in earlier times would have been labelled as 'pagan'. The 'profane' will be what the convert has to renounce in undergoing conversion. 'Secular' does not have such connotations of radical opposition to the sacred; it is more

13. Cf., e.g., the French Conseil d'État's *Rapport public: Un siècle de laïcité* (2004): 'Intraduisible dans la plupart des langues, le concept de laïcité renvoie, au sens large, à une perte d'emprise de la religion sur la société. Plus précisément, la laïcité française signifie le refus de l'assujettissement du politique au religieux, ou réciproquement, sans qu'il y ait forcément étanchéité totale de l'un et de l'autre. Elle implique la reconnaissance du pluralisme religieux et de la neutralité de l'État vis à vis des Églises.' Cf. Henri Peña-Ruiz, *Qu'est-ce que la laïcité?* (Paris, 2003).

14. E.g., René Rémond, *Religion et société en Europe et la sécularisation aux XIXe et XXe siècles, 1789–2000* (Paris, 2001).

15. On this, see P. F. Beatrice, 'On the Meaning of *bebelos-profanus* in the Pagan-Christian Conflict of the Fourth Century' (paper presented at the Atelier sur les frontières du profane dans l'Empire romain pendant l'Antiquité tardive: III—Les groupes religieux et les frontières du profane, École française de Rome, Rome, 23–24 April 2004).

neutral, capable of being accepted or adapted: the domain of the religious—though not moral—*adiaphora*. It will be the shared overlap between insider and outsider groups, the sphere in which they can have a common interest and which—from the Christian point of view—need not be repudiated or excluded. It can be spoken of without reference to religion, whereas both 'sacred' and 'profane', in this usage, will necessarily involve some reference to religion.[16]

It is easy to misunderstand the neutrality implied in secularity. A great deal of misunderstanding arises from failure to distinguish the private from the public realm. The neutrality which is an essential aspect of the secular—no discrimination between religions, worldviews, ideologies—is a requirement in the public sphere. Thus, for instance, it has been said that 'secular community has no ground *of its own* on which it may simply exist apart. It is either opened up to its fulfilment in God's love, or it is shut down.'[17] The truth of such a statement depends entirely on being understood to refer strictly to the public realm of the community. A truly secular community does not have grounds *of its own* (understood as ultimate religious or ontological foundations); such grounds belong to the private sphere of its members and are excluded from the public realm. Modern defences of a secular society, of *laïcité*, would insist on its complete openness to and inclusiveness of diversity.[18]

What is comprehended within the public realm is what is common to all the members of the community; by implication, it can be spoken of without reference to religion, which, *ex hypothesi*, is not common to them. In other words, from the Christian point of view, the secular is roughly equivalent to what can be shared with non-Christians. In a society where Christians rub shoulders with others, one possible way of defining what is secular is to point to what can be shared with non-Christians. This is possible only so long as we are dealing with a society which lacks religious homogeneity. It obviously ceases to be possible in a society that is virtually totally Christian.

16. I have used the term in this sense, for instance, in Markus, *Saeculum*, 122. Cf. Markus, *End of Ancient Christianity*, esp. 13–14, 134.

17. Oliver O'Donovan, *Common Objects of Love: Moral Reflection and the Shaping of Community* (Cambridge, 2002), 24 (italics mine).

18. E.g., by Peña-Ruiz, *Qu'est-ce que la laïcité?* This theme is discussed at length in chap. 3.

The two ways of defining the secular that I am suggesting seem to be related to the two meanings of 'secularism' distinguished by Charles Taylor.[19] Taking the Wars of Religion of the seventeenth century, 'or rather, the search in battle-fatigue and horror for a way out of them' (32), as the starting point of modern Western secularism, Taylor distinguishes two forms of secularism as alternative exit strategies from such a situation of conflict. The first, 'the common ground strategy', assumes a certain range of beliefs shared by all Christians (or all theists) and minimises or eliminates confessional differences that lie outside the boundaries of this shared ground. The second tries to define 'an independent political ethic', a strategy he associates with Hugo Grotius. This abstracts 'from our religious beliefs altogether' and establishes norms, including norms for how human beings should behave towards one another in society, on which to found a public morality independent of grounds based on religious belief. It is able to provide an area 'immune from [sic] all these warring beliefs' (33–34), excluding these by confining them to a private sphere.

Taylor goes on to consider the problem which arises within the first model, when the area of common ground shrinks to exclude religion altogether, as it does in many modern pluralist societies. I am not concerned here with the way he proposes of dealing with the problem. Rather, I would suggest that the two models shade into each other, in proportion to the extent that a given society lacks religious homogeneity. When all confessional differences are eliminated from the public realm, the shared sphere remaining may include common Christian (or theistic) features shared by them. If so, the residual common ground between them will include some Christian (or religious) elements. If the heterogeneity embraces non-Christian groups, as it now does in much of Western Europe and North America (and elsewhere), all that can be shared is a reduced, nonreligious, common ground; and that will be in effect equivalent to the 'independent political ethic'.[20] Given sufficient diversity, at the limit, the highest common factor shared by virtually all within the society, whatever their religious affiliations, will coincide with what can be established without reference to religion.

19. Charles Taylor, 'Modes of Secularism', in *Secularism and Its Critics*, ed. Rajeev Bhargava (New Delhi, 1998), 31–53. Further citations to this work are given parenthetically in the text.

20. This will turn out to have close relations to John Rawls's conception of 'justice as fairness', which I consider in chap. 3.

In other words, the two models may be different in principle: the 'independent political ethic' strategy seeks to construct a political ethic from the ground up, so to speak, without reference to any religious basis, whereas the 'common ground' model works from the top down, excluding as much religious reference as is peculiar to one or more groups but not generally shared within the community. But the difference in practise implied by the two models is a matter of degree, depending on the range of religious and moral diversity that obtains at any given time. The bounds of consensus will shrink in proportion to the extent of religious heterogeneity within the community and broaden in proportion to the extent of religious homogeneity. At the limit, in a society which is virtually homogeneous in respect of its religion, the first way of defining what is secular would cease to be applicable.

This is just what came into being in the course of the emergence of Western Christendom from Roman Late Antiquity—a 'desecularisation' which is the reverse of what happened in the Wars of Religion. If a notion of the secular were to apply in such a society, it would have to be defined in more problematic terms: as what does not form part of a religious discourse. To define a secular sphere, the members of a 'Christian society' would have, so to speak, to imagine the kind of consensus that could be achieved if their Christianity were not virtually universally shared in their society. In Roman society, right down at any rate to the sixth century—which, as I shall suggest in my last chapter, is the watershed in this respect—the reverse was the case, as it is in our modern industrial societies.

It must be evident that any discussion of the secular will impinge at many points on a number of controversial political and theological topics. Among theologians the trend towards a 'secular theology' has lost much of its appeal and has given way to theological perspectives hostile to it: not only in the Barthian tradition, but in the work of the theologians claiming the designation of 'radical orthodoxy', in the attacks on 'Constantinianism' of John Howard Yoder, and in the work of distinguished moral theologians such as Stanley Hauerwas and Oliver O'Donovan.[21] Much of the argument of this book will in fact turn out to be an implicit dialogue, often indeed made explicit, with some of these thinkers. Oliver O'Donovan's great work

---

21. Cf. the opening sentence of Song's *Christianity and Liberal Society:* 'Ever since Karl Barth's inversion of nineteenth-century cultural Protestantism in the early decades of the twentieth century, the predominant attitude of Christian theology towards its surrounding culture has been one of critical distance rather than uncritical legitimation.'

The Desire of the Nations[22] has especially been a constant intellectual challenge as well as a source of inspiration, and I have frequently had to find my way of coming to terms with the views propounded there, sometimes by following the signposts, more often by distancing myself from them.

The core of my argument in this book can be briefly summarised. Its substance is that Christian tradition has a legitimate place for the autonomy of the secular, even though for many centuries this was eclipsed in its awareness, and despite the perpetual undertow of what we have become accustomed to call 'triumphalism' in Christian political and cultural attitudes. (By 'triumphalism' I mean approving, supporting, or, in their absence, hankering after the conditions which allow institutional religious influence or domination to bear on the legal, cultural, or political structures within the surrounding society; or, put another way, the inclination to approve the subjection of a society's culture or its legal or political institutions to religious groups or their views. My use of the term has affinities, without being quite synonymous, with what French theorists call *intégrisme*,[23] as well as with what some theologians have called 'Constantinianism'.[24]

In the first chapter I begin with the roots of the notion of a secular realm in the New Testament, and its emergence and fortunes in the early centuries down to the time of Constantine and the Christian Roman Empire. In the period between the apostolic age and Constantine the problem of the relation between Christianity and a secular society and its culture was suppressed for Christians, being in effect taken out of their hands. They saw themselves as sharply distinct in, if not separate from, the society and culture of their non-Christian fellows, marked off by boundaries imposed on them, not of their own but of outsiders' making. Dominating this society and its culture was not even an unrealistic option. The 'Constantinian settlement' changed the situation radically and raised the problem in an acute form. I see this and its sequel, the new conditions engendered by the gradual Christianisation of the Roman Empire, as the great divide in Christian history. I discuss this theme in the second part of my first chapter and consider

22. Oliver O'Donovan, *The Desire of the Nations: Rediscovering the Roots of Political Theology* (Oxford, 1996).

23. See, e.g., Peña-Ruiz, *Qu'est-ce que la laïcité?*: 'qui d'une certaine norme religieuse veut faire une loi politique' (129). The term is, of course, often used in a sense more akin to 'fundamentalism'.

24. On this, see chap. 1.

how Christians confronted the problem of adjusting themselves to the culture and society of the Empire.

In the second chapter I go on to consider the response of Augustine of Hippo, whom I continue to take to be the outstanding critic of the ideology of the Christian Empire as it had developed by the end of the fourth century and in the time of the Theodosian emperors. In the third chapter I seek to defend my view that Augustine, while far from indifferent to the moral foundations of his society, was the principal Christian thinker to defend a place for the secular within a religious, Christian interpretation of the world and of history.

In these two middle chapters I ask, first, going back more specifically to Augustine himself: Does he still look the same now, over thirty years later, as he did at the time when I interpreted his thought—often with less caution than would have been advisable—at the height of the enthusiasm for secularity, as legitimating the secular? This is one of the central themes I shall deal with in these two chapters. My main purpose will not be to reply to criticism, some of it penetrating and very much to the point, of the views I propounded then. I shall indeed have occasion to try to answer some of the objections raised, but only incidentally to my central purpose: What sort of view of human society in relation to the Kingdom of God would an appeal to an *Augustinus redivivus* authorise? I try to reassess Augustine's position in relation to a number of concerns that have surfaced and become significant in theological and historical discussion as well as in the field of political theory since the 1950s and 1960s. It will be obvious that the kind of preoccupations which have shaped thinking about liberalism in recent decades lurk in the background of my thinking about Augustine.[25] The place of religion in society, the idea of a secular society, and cognate issues—political pluralism, multiculturalism, problems of group and cultural identity, toleration, and the like—all these, along with what has been called the 'Enlightenment project', have been extensively debated, criticised, and re-

25. I am conscious of the risk of the word 'liberal' being misunderstood, especially in the United States. When I use it, especially in chap. 3, I have in mind the tradition of political thought from John Stuart Mill to Isaiah Berlin and John Rawls. Song has rightly remarked in *Christianity and Liberal Society* that liberalism is a diffuse phenomenon, with 'no common or unitary core doctrine' (40) but with sufficient family likeness to allow us to group together 'thinkers who are disparate but still sufficiently close to enable us to point to a pattern of characteristic family resemblances' (9–10). Cf. Basil Mitchell, *Law, Morality and Religion in a Secular Society* (Oxford, 1967), 87–102.

stated by philosophers, political thinkers, sociologists, and cultural anthro-
pologists, as well as theologians, from several points of view in the decades
since 1970. In interpreting Augustine's legacy I shall need to touch on these
debates as occasion arises and to take them into account, if only marginally.

The final chapter traces the increasingly religious orientation of Roman
society and its culture, especially from the second half of the sixth century,
and the eclipse of the secular at the end of antiquity and during the Christian Middle Ages in Western Europe.[26] I shall go on—very briefly—to reflect
on its rehabilitation, above all by the Blessed Pope John XXIII, in whose
honour these lectures have been instituted, and the second Vatican Council.[27] The council has, in this respect as in so many others, been a watershed
for Catholic thinking. Many educated Catholics brought up in the generations which preceded it inevitably felt the tension between their Catholic
loyalties and the Western culture shared with their Christian, and beyond
them, non-Christian, fellows. It could almost seem as if they were required
to turn their backs on a century or more of European cultural development
between Pius IX and Pius XII. Pope John's vision can be seen, and could be
experienced, as a liberation from a Catholic cultural ghetto. It amounted to
an acknowledgement of the secular as an autonomous realm. In this book

26. I am unable to deal with the theme in Eastern Europe, or indeed in the wider
world. It is also very likely that the problems about the secular are peculiar to Christianity
in its Western versions.

27. A claim has been made on behalf of John Paul II by his biographer to his being
the pope responsible for bringing to an end the 'Constantinian' period of Christianity. According to him John Paul II was the champion of a way of conceiving a Western ideal
which gives pluralism and secularity a central role. He is cast for the role of the pope who
has made the most decisive break with Constantinianism:

> If by 'Constantinian Church' we mean a church that was fully participant in public life
> but that tended to accept many of the canons of public life as 'the world' defined
> them, it might be argued that John Paul II has been developing a 'post-Constantinian'
> model for twenty-first-century Catholicism. . . . It is a church that . . . has reacquired a
> certain critical distance from the worlds of power, precisely in order to help hold those
> worlds accountable to universal moral norms. . . . [It] no longer seeks, and in fact flatly
> rejects, the mantle of coercive power as a buttress to its evangelical mission.

George Weigel, 'Roman Catholicism in the Age of John Paul II', in Berger, *Desecularization
of the World*, 32.

I consider the Blessed Pope John XXIII and the second Vatican Council at the end of
chap. 4.

I try to place this achievement into a Christian tradition reaching back at least to Augustine of Hippo.

*

The subject of this book has been the central preoccupation of most of my work over some forty years. The book has given me the opportunity to pull together some of the threads and to offer some reconsiderations. I have indicated in footnotes other publications where I have dealt with one or another point under discussion in greater depth or detail, as well as points on which I have changed my mind (especially in chapter 3) in consequence of further thought, discussion, or criticism. Otherwise, except, of course, for the notes, the text printed here is a slightly expanded version of the lectures as they were given.

*

The University of Notre Dame has provided the occasion and the stimulus for this process of rethinking. I am deeply grateful to the university, and especially to John Cavadini, for inviting me to give these Blessed Pope John XXIII lectures, helping me to define their theme, and, in so doing, spurring me to undertake a task that I had long shied away from. No setting could be more congenial to this work than that of a Christian academic community dedicated to the pursuit of the intellectual life of the greatest rigour. Having already visited Notre Dame and having once spent a semester there, I was glad to accept the invitation, and I am grateful for the generous hospitality I enjoyed. The lectures were made possible by the generosity of Robert L. Dilenschneider and his family.

Next to Notre Dame, my greatest debt is to Éric Rebillard and Claire Sotinel and the series of seminars they organised in 2003 and 2004 under the auspices of the École française de Rome, 'Les frontières du profane dans l'Empire romain pendant l'Antiquité tardive', which have provided much stimulating material for thought. Individual contributions are acknowledged in their proper places. I have also profited from the comments of friends—especially Claire Sotinel, Jean Porter, and Robert Dodaro—whose ways of thinking did not always, by any means, coincide with mine.

1

FROM THE BEGINNINGS TO THE
CHRISTIAN EMPIRE

The idea of the secular is present within the Christian tradition from the
start but takes on a very different meaning according to the historical circumstances in which it is applied. Nowadays, for instance, it has gotten inextricably mixed up with discussions of the role of lay people.[1] I shall argue
that some notion of a secular realm is an essential constituent of Christian
belief but that its content is variable, contingent upon the historical circumstances. These circumstances are determined, in my view, by two sets of fac-
tors: on the one hand, the conditions under which the Christian community
lives in the surrounding society, and on the other, the attitudes prevailing
within the Christian community towards that society and its culture and its
own relation to it. From both these contingencies it follows that what is considered secular will depend on place as well as time.

In this chapter I trace the major mutations that the secular underwent in
relation to the changes in the conditions of Christianity in the world around
it in the first three and a half centuries. I begin with a look at the roots of
the notion in the New Testament. I then go on to locate Christianity on the

---

1. See, for instance, Paul Lakeland, *The Liberation of the Laity: In Search of an
Accountable Church* (New York, 2003), esp. 149–85. Ancient usage of *saecularis* is no less
varied. For wider discussion, see the Introduction.

religious map of the Roman Empire, among the other religions, during the period before it was singled out for special favour and, eventually, public recognition. In the final part of this chapter I sketch the impact of Constantine—the major watershed in its history—and the emergence of the problem of secularity in the new conditions created by the Christianisation of the Empire in the time following Constantine.

The term 'secular' is foreign to early Christian language, but it derives from one that is very familiar: *saeculum (aiôn)*, a term at the core of the New Testament's affirmation that in Christ a new age has dawned over the present age, this *saeculum*. The secular is that which belongs to this age and will have no part in the age to come, when Christ's kingship will hold universal sway. Political authority and institutions, with all the agencies of compulsion and enforcement, are destined for abrogation when the rule of God in Christ is finally revealed.[2] Until then, however, they retain their place in the divine plan. What Pauline theology speaks of is their limitation in time and to history, rather than any limitation in their scope . Between the incarnation of Christ and His *parousia,* the 'powers' of this world minister to God and continue to exercise their sway (Rom. 13:6); they are still visible, still active, and—it is important to be clear—still legitimate, although in principle they have been overcome in Christ's victory and are now subject to Him. They have been, not destroyed, but dethroned, kept on a short leash.[3]

The Swiss theologian Oscar Cullmann has stressed the duality of Christ's lordship in Pauline theology: 'Only in the Kingdom of God will there no longer be two realms, for there God will be "all in all".'[4] The relationship between Christ's lordship over the Church and his lordship over the world has been schematically represented by two concentric circles. An inner circle, in which his rule has been fully established, represents the Church, Christ's body, which consists of His members, who acknowledge and proclaim His lordship. It is surrounded by a larger circle, the world, to which His lordship

---

2. Cf. Oliver O'Donovan, *The Desire of the Nations: Rediscovering the Roots of Political Theology* (Oxford, 1996), 211–12. Further citations to this work are given parenthetically in the text.

3. Hendrik Berkhof, *Christ and the Powers,* trans. John Howard Yoder (Scottdale, PA., 1962), 39–43. Cf. Oscar Cullmann, *Christ and Time: The Primitive Christian Conception of Time and History,* trans. Floyd V. Filson (London, 1951), and *The State in the New Testament* (London, 1963), 54–55. For further discussion, see 'Additional Note on Secular Powers' in this chapter, pp. 28–30.

4. Cullmann, *Christ and Time,* 208, cf. 199.

is proclaimed but where it is yet to be fully acknowledged and rendered visible.[5] This outer ring, destined to disappear at the end but not to be prematurely encroached on, is the sphere of the secular.

Christianity is committed—perhaps uniquely among world religions—to a belief in a Church—that is, a visible community of believers distinct from political society. The two will always overlap but never coincide. The inner circle, the Church, is the sacramental anticipation of the future Kingdom which it is charged to proclaim to the world. The outer circle is the secular, the realm which is still in a state of waiting for the proclamation to be heard and received. It may be wider or it may be narrower; but it will always be there until the eschaton. The visible Church, we might say, proclaims, anticipates, and shows forth as a sacramental sign the full realisation of God's kingdom to be revealed at the end.[6] There will always be an 'eschatological gap' between proclamation of the message and submission to it.

Generations of exegetes have taught us to appreciate the complexity of the New Testament's attitude to what they have called, justifiably, though perhaps unwisely giving hostages to fortune, 'the state'.[7] Its ambivalence towards the secular power structures, institutions, and relationships rests on the ambivalence towards the 'powers':[8] on the one hand, they are part of God's good creation and play a part in His providential plan; on the other hand, by a demonic reversal of their role, they separate men from God. The

---

5. Cullmann, *Christ and Time*, 188–208. On defining the 'secular', see O'Donovan, *Desire of the Nations*, 211–12.

6. Most recently, Oliver O'Donovan, in *Common Objects of Love: Moral Reflection and the Shaping of Community* (Cambridge, 2000), has also emphasised this eschatological character of secularity: 'The Christian conception of the "secularity" of political society arose directly out of this Jewish wrestling with unfulfilled promise,' and 'Secularity is irreducibly an eschatological notion; it requires an eschatological faith to sustain it, a belief in a disclosure that is "not yet"' (24). Cf. 'Secularity is a stance of patience in the face of plurality' (63).

7. They are frequently reprimanded for doing so (e.g., by O'Donovan, *Desire of the Nations*, 152, 231–33), on the grounds that to speak of 'the state' is anachronistic and that neither Greek nor Latin contains any equivalent term. This charge, though strictly speaking correct, is, however, unwarranted: what is normally meant by scholars who do use 'the state' in this context is roughly the equivalent of what 'the state' means in modern English (cf. again the 'functions' spelt out by O'Donovan in *Desire of the Nations*).

8. E.g., Cullmann, *State in the New Testament*, passim, and *Christ and Time*, 199–205. On the double reference of the word to secular authorities and invisible, demonic, powers, see *State in the New Testament*, 51–52, and *Christ and Time*, 191–210.

fallen and rebellious agencies which hold human beings in thrall, separating them from the love of God (Rom. 8:38), in servitude (Col. 2:20; Gal. 4:3), are, however, 'still the framework of creation, preserving it from disintegration.'[9] In this fallen world, they are necessary to the continuance of social life. They stand behind the solid structures which form the scaffolding of human societies; apart from Christ, we are at their mercy. But for all that, they are forces 'which hold together the world and the life of men and preserve them from chaos',[10] and the Christian community has continued down the centuries to pray 'for kings and for all that are in authority; that we may lead a quiet and peaceable life in all godliness and harmony' (1 Tim. 2:2).[11]

Even some of the most radical modern theologians have recognised the continuing validity of the present dispensation with its institutions and agencies, while, of course, also stressing their potential for perversion and rebellion.[12] The powers of this world are poised between the eschatological Kingdom and the realm of Satan or the Antichrist, and they have a choice between serving the one or the other. By claiming absolute powers not subject to God's authority, by usurping quasi-divine prerogative over human beings, in short, by seeking to escape the conditions imposed by the triumph of Christ's cross over them, they betray the purpose for which they are sanctioned. This was precisely the situation which the author of the Book of Revelation sought to integrate into his Christian vision of history. His

---

9. Berkhof, *Christ and the Powers*, 30.

10. Berkhof, *Christ and the Powers*, 22. On some implications, see, e.g., Walter Wink, *Engaging the Powers: Discernment and Resistance in a World of Domination* (Minneapolis, 1992).

11. See especially Gerd Tellenbach, 'Römischer und christlicher Reichsgedanke in der Liturgie des Mittelalters', *Heidelberg Akademie der Wissenschaften, Philosophisch-historische Klasse*, 1934–35, 3–71. Reprinted in Gerd Tellenbach, *Ausgewählte Abhandlungen und Aufsätze* (Stuttgart, 1988), 2:343–410.

12. John Howard Yoder, for instance, states in *The Original Revolution: Essays on Christian Pacifism* (Scottdale, PA, 1971) that Rom. 13:1, Tim. 2 and 1 Peter 2 give criteria for judging state's activities. 'If the use of force is such as to protect the innocent and punish evildoers to preserve peace so that "all men might come to knowledge of the truth," then that state may be considered as fitting within God's plan, as subject to the reign of Christ' (63). (I return to this quotation in chap. 3, n. 19.) Cf. John Howard Yoder, *The Politics of Jesus: Vicit Agnus Noster* (Grand Rapids, MI, 1972), 190–92, and *Original Revolution*, 142–50, on Pauline 'exousiology'. His discussion of the 'rights of the state' in *Politics of Jesus*, 193–214, however, seems to run counter to this recognition, as pointed out by O'Donovan, *Desire of the Nations*, 151–52.

apocalyptic image of the Roman Empire is in no way contrary to the positive value set upon government in general in Romans 13 or 1 Peter 2:13–15.[13] John Howard Yoder has put this most powerfully: 'The essential change which has taken place is not within the realm of the old aeon, vengeance and the state, where there is really no change; it is rather that the new aeon revealed in Christ takes primacy over the old, explains the meaning of the old, and will finally vanquish the old. The state did not change with the coming of Christ; what changed was the coming of the new aeon which proclaimed the doom of the old one.'[14] Until the consummation of that doom, the secular realm retains its legitimate place in the divine order. Secularity, in Oliver O'Donovan's words, is 'the stance of patience in the face of plurality',[15] with what is 'out there'. And that is what the Christian communities needed above all in the first three centuries of their existence.

It is not hard to understand why the Pauline image of the 'powers of this world' should be readily utilised to provide a basis for defining the place of political authority in the Church's perspective—why theologians would found a doctrine of Church and state, or a distinction between their respective functions as sacred and secular, on this conceptual pair, especially in times of confrontation with totalitarian regimes. The conflict between the Church and the secular powers under the National Socialist regime in Germany, for instance, helped to focus the attention of theologians and New Testament scholars on this theme, especially just before and after the Second World War. Then, as in the Apostolic Church and in the early Christian period, the need was for some limit that could be set to the public authority's reach into the life of the Church's communal witness and worship.

The boundary, however, was, and is always, porous and far from fixed. During the first two and a half centuries of its existence, the Christian Church and Roman society around it perceived each other as mutually alien. In the pre-Constantinian world the Church stood out as a sharply defined group. A century ago the great ecclesiastical historian Adolf von Harnack commented on the designation of Christians, common in the early centuries, as 'the third race' *(tertium genus)*: 'It is indeed amazing! One had certainly no idea that in the consciousness of the Greeks and Romans the Jews stood out in such bold relief from the other nations, and the Christians from

---

13. Cf. O'Donovan, *Desire of the Nations*, 152–53.
14. Yoder, *Original Revolution*, 62–63.
15. Cf. O'Donovan, *Common Objects of Love*, 63.

both, that they represented themselves as independent "genera", and were so described in an explicit formula. Neither Jews nor Christians could look for a more ample recognition, little as the demarcation was intended as a recognition at all.'[16] Christians were a group set apart from their world, whose suppression, haphazard or organised, could even help to define a pagan identity. And Christians could feel themselves as outsiders, with a cliquish subculture of their own, obeying their own norms, upholding their own distinct standards, alienated from the secular culture and its values, to which they owed only very limited debts. *Extranei a turbis aestimemur,* 'We are seen as outsiders', as the Christian writer Tertullian said.[17] If from the outside Christians were a 'lurking breed which avoids the light of day',[18] they, from their side, saw their community as clearly marked off from the world around them: an alien world, which had to be put up with, suffered in patience. It was not necessarily hostile, and was sometimes even seen as potentially a partner, but predominantly it was a society in which the boundary between the Church and what lay outside it was very clearly marked. If nothing else identified the Christian community as separate from the Roman world around it, it was amply marked out by the ring-fence of suspicion, calumny, and liability to intermittent persecution and pogrom. The whole world conspired to define the Christians as a visibly identifiable group[19] in secular society, of the type often referred to as a 'sect'.

Even in a world in which the Christian community was seen, and saw itself, as a sect, the problem of demarcating a realm of the secular from the

16. Adolf von Harnack, *The Expansion of Christianity in the First Three Centuries,* ed. and trans. James Moffat (London, 1904), 1:349. On this, see Robert A. Markus, 'The Problem of Self-Definition: From Sect to Church', in *Jewish and Christian Self-Definition,* vol. 1, *The Shaping of Christianity in the Second and Third Centuries,* ed. E. P. Sanders (London, 1980), 1–15, 217–19; reprinted in Robert A. Markus, *From Augustine to Gregory the Great: History and Christianity in Late Antiquity* (London, 1983), article I. On the use of ethnic categories, see D. K. Buell, 'Race and Universalism in Early Christianity', *Journal of Early Christian Studies* 10 (2002): 429–68. For an excellent recent account, see Richard A. Norris Jr., 'Articulating Identity', in *The Cambridge History of Early Christian Literature,* ed. Frances M. Young, Lewis Ayres, and Andrew Louth (Cambridge, 2004), 71–90.

17. Tertullian, *Apol.* 31.

18. Minucius Felix, *Oct.* 8.

19. In speaking of a 'group', I would of course wish to be understood to refer to a large number of local groups. For further discussion, see 'Additional Note on Church and Sect' in this chapter, p. 30.

profane—that is, between what might be acceptable and what would have to be repudiated—could not be avoided. As Tertullian well knew and sometimes said, Christians shared a great deal with their non-Christian neighbours. Equally, however, there were large and crucially important areas of life in which their views and values clashed, and there were areas of uncertainty and contention: Should Christians go to the shows *(spectacula)*? Should they bear arms? Enjoy pagan literature, or cultivate an interest in philosophy? What was acceptable and could be shared with pagans would lie within the secular; what lay beyond that boundary would be proscribed as irredeemably pagan or profane. In the generations following Tertullian's this proscribed area would shrink drastically in size. But until the advent of the first Christian emperor, the barriers, even if lowered, remained in place.

Christianity was a religion in a sense different from the religions hitherto admissible in the Roman world. The religions of the Empire catered to different needs and overlapped only in part with what the Christian Church offered to its members. As A. D. Nock, the great scholar of Greek and Roman religions, observed: 'The Jew and the Christian offered religions as we understand religion; the others offered cults. But their contemporaries did not expect anything more than cults from them and looked to philosophy for guidance in conduct and for a scheme of the Universe. . . . Worship had no key to life's meaning: that was offered by philosophy.'[20] Christianity—to leave aside now its parent, Judaism—offered its adherents both a cult and a philosophy. It gave a key to the meaning of life and the universe, and it provided a rule of conduct as well as worship in the spirit and the truth. (Augustine thought—perhaps following a hint from Lactantius—that the special claim of Christianity rested on this integration of cult and truth, overcoming the ancient cleavage between them.)[21] It made an exclusive claim to truth and validated a vision of human life alternative to that of the traditional public cults of Rome. Until the advent of Constantine it was inevitably an outsider religion, excluded by the nature of its claims. But this was to change in the fourth century.

20. Arthur Darby Nock, *Conversion: The Old and the New in Religion from Alexander the Great to Augustine of Hippo* (Oxford, 1933), 16, 163.

21. Augustine, *De vera rel.* 4.8. The theme of the divorce between philosophy and true wisdom is common in Lactantius, and traces of his *Institutes* abound in Augustine's *De vera religione*. This is the underlying theme of his attack on pagan religion in the *De civitate Dei* 2.6–7 and of the three Varronic 'theologies' in *De civitate Dei* 6.5.

No modern scholar has written more illuminatingly on this subject than John North. I quote him:

> The communities in the archaic Greco-Roman world, whether they were based on city-states or on tribal systems, or were incorporated in larger imperial associations, had their own specific form of religious life. In this form, religious rituals and practices were integral to all civic, local or family activities; and religious roles, sometimes overlapping with political ones, were ubiquitous. But there were no differentiated religious institutions or identifiable religious groups based on popular membership. There was thus no question of religion providing the individual or the group with a system of power or adherence, alternative to that of the city, the tribe, or the family. . . . On the other hand, in some sense all groups in the pagan world were religious, since they all involved some degree of cultic and religious activity, some orientation to the gods.[22]

Of course there was a wide variety of religions, cults, and philosophical schools in the Greco-Roman world. But they were not generally in competition, not rival bidders for their followers' loyalties. They were often mutually compatible without much difficulty and, what is more important, compatible with the ritual practises of the public cult. For their followers, they were not alternatives to civic religion but additions to it. The hospitality of traditional Roman religion to cults rooted in distant provinces naturally broadened in the centuries after Augustus. Especially from the Severan period, when Roman conservatism in religious matters softened—to the extent that Tertullian lamented its withering, wryly commenting on the free rein given to Serapis and Bacchus 'against the authority of ancient tradition'[23]—even newfangled cults imported from outlying regions could find a home in Rome. Its tolerance was not unrestricted, but the relation between Rome and its empire involved a wide spectrum of religions and stretched the limits of the acceptable.[24]

22. John North, 'The Development of Religious Pluralism', in *The Jews among Pagans and Christians: In the Roman Empire*, ed. Judith Lieu, John North, and Tessa Rajak (London, 1992), 177.

23. Tertullian, *Apol.* 6.

24. A good account is to be found in Mary Beard, John North, and Simon Price, *Religions of Rome*, 2 vols. (Cambridge University Press, 1998), esp. 1:211–363. See also P. Garnsey, 'Religious Toleration in Classical Antiquity', *Studies in Church History* 21 (1984): 1–27.

Within these limits, however,[25] the cults current in the Empire could co-exist fairly peacefully. Some cults may have found it hard to gain admission into the Empire, but Judaism and Christianity were the two major exceptions. Both were resistant to being brought within the scope of this symbiosis. Judaism, although the adherence of proselytes and sympathetic outsiders would in the course of time blur its largely ethnic boundaries, remained defined mainly by descent. Christianity, as it gradually ceased to be seen as a breakaway Jewish sect, was for three hundred years felt to be a foreign body in Roman society. Neither religion was an option for most Romans; and both would have recoiled in horror from being combined with civic 'paganism'.

At first hated as the religion of a suspect and outlandish minority, in the course of the third century Christianity gradually lost this character. By the end of the century, though still a minority religion, it was much larger and much less outlandish, and though still hated, it was hated in a new and different way: it had now begun to appeal to and, along with its appeal, to divide the educated townsmen who ran the Empire. It numbered adherents from all classes in its ranks; its social composition is likely to have reflected a good cross section of Roman urban society.[26] While many were being won over to Christianity, others saw it as a challenge to the traditional role of paganism in Roman society. In the Great Persecution at the beginning of the fourth century, the forces of Roman conservatism rallied in a last attempt to eliminate a dangerous threat to the traditional consensus. During the eighty or so years beginning with Constantine coming to power over the Empire after the famous battle he won in 312 with the aid, as he believed, of the God of the Christians, and ending with the enforcement of Christian orthodoxy under Theodosius I in the 390s, Christianity became the established, respectable, patronised, and, in the end, officially enforced religion of the Roman Empire.

Constantine's victory and his assumption of control in the West changed the situation radically. It ushered in the major revolution in the Church's mode of existence in the world, which I will consider later. For the moment we must consider its more immediate result. The 'great thaw' inaugurated by the advent of Constantine created a situation which has been likened (in

25. Cf. North, 'Development of Religious Pluralism', 180–83, with criticism of the views put forward by Walter Burkert, *Ancient Mystery Cults* (Cambridge, MA, 1987).

26. I have described this development in Robert A. Markus, *Christianity in the Roman World* (London, 1974), 70–86 ('Towards Respectability').

the language of Peter Berger) to a marketplace in religions. The result was that by the early fourth century 'the official cults of Rome, once a traditional set of practises embedded unproblematically in a stable social order, had become one option among many'.[27] The resulting pluralisation destroyed the original situation: Roman society as a whole no longer authenticated a single shared conception of the cosmos.[28] Instead of religions embedded in the city-state, what we have in the post-Constantinian Empire are religions as a 'choice of differentiated groups offering different qualities of religious doctrine, different experiences, insights, or just different myths and stories to make sense of human experience.'[29]

The neutrality apparently upheld in the 'edict' issued by Constantine and Licinius soon after Constantine's victory in 312, a neutrality unprecedented in Roman history—and destined to be short-lived—brought Christianity into the marketplace of religions and transformed the nature of the competition. Christianity, it seems alone among all the new cults, claimed an exclusivity which necessarily implied treating all other cults as rivals.[30] Voluntary choice between alternative religious affiliations and, along with it, competition and conflict among religious groups had come to replace the earlier civic religion. Religious choice was embodied in voluntary adherence to defined groups, with their own structures of authority. The gradual developments of the third century now came to a climax in a wholly new situation: one in which chosen religious commitment, and voluntary belonging to groups defined in terms of religious adherence, came to supersede religious loyalties to the gods of the city, or of the Empire that had come increasingly to take an interest in its citizens' religions. And Christianity was now a major competitor in the marketplace, newly liberated and able to compete on a level playing field (not that it remained level for very long: it was soon to tilt steeply in Christianity's favour).

This brings me to the final part of this chapter and to what will be a central thread of this book, the difference made by Constantine to the notion of the secular. The Constantinian revolution—a process which I take to be more or less co-extensive with the 'long fourth century', stretching from around AD 250 to 450—transformed the way Christians saw themselves in their world. To avoid any doubt, let me make it clear that I use the phrase to

27. Beard, North, and Price, *Religions of Rome*, 1:312.
28. North, 'Development of Religious Pluralism', 178–79.
29. North, 'Development of Religious Pluralism', 178.
30. Beard, North, and Price, *Religions of Rome*, 1:310.

refer to a revolution in the Church's way of being in the world, not to a revolution in the Roman Empire. This transformation of its relationship to the world around it amounts to one of the most decisive of the *caesurae* in the whole of the Church's history. But what concerns us more directly here is the transformation in the meaning of the secular that came with it and, indeed, gave the notion its importance for the first time: the question about the secular was bound up with the sense of a Christian identity.

For hitherto, in the first two and a half centuries or so, there had been no urgent necessity for defining a realm of the secular. What was distinctive about Christianity in this surrounding social order? What could be shared with non-Christians? What was absolutely opposed to a Christian commitment? These questions had been less urgent while Christianity was an excluded, well-defined minority in the surrounding society. There had been quite enough that Christians did not share with non-Christians to mark them out among their fellows. Now, however, the impetus towards sharing in what had long been regarded as peculiar to pagans was irresistible. As the area of what they shared continued to grow inexorably, the need to define the boundaries that demarcated the Church from what lay outside became more urgent. The world was flowing into the Church, being taken over wholesale by the Church, and the Church was expanding its influence into more and more areas of the culture of Roman society and dominating ever-growing areas of its daily life. What some theologians have labelled 'Constantinianism'[31] transformed the Church's position in the world.

This story has been often told, and I need only remind you of its central thrust. Christianity was now tied to the Empire, to which breaches in the Church's unity came to seem a threat and any divisions a matter of concern. The affairs of the Church became a matter of interest to the government; the clergy, unless they belonged to one of the groups classed as heretical or schismatic, on the whole accepted the government's involvement in its affairs. With the conversion of the emperors to Christianity and the flow of imperial favour and of privilege, prestige, and wealth, earlier opposition and hesitations vanished almost overnight, except in fringe groups officially

---

31. For a brief critique of the Protestant theological tradition on this question, largely confined, however, to the limited and crude version according to which the Church's doctrinal development was shaped by imperial policy rather than by its own dynamic, see D. H. Williams, 'Constantine, Nicaea and the "Fall" of the Church', in *Christian Origins: Theology, Rhetoric and Community*, ed. Lewis Ayres and Gareth Jones (London, 1998), 117–36.

deemed to be dissident. The lay elites, educated (as before, but now more widely) in the same schools as their non-Christian fellows, came to adhere to the same shared values and adopted the current artistic styles, literary traditions, and lifestyles. Many of them rose in the social and official hierarchy to positions of power and responsibility and began to have a stake and unprecedented status in secular society. Bishops in their sermons and poets in their imagery instinctively represented the Empire as the divinely willed medium of Christian existence; Christianity and 'Romanity' became coextensive and were seen as providentially designed for each other. Christianity had come to be closely identified with being Roman. It was hard to imagine a non-Roman form of Christianity—so hard that one Christian writer thought God had to bring the barbarians into the Roman territories in order to make the gospel available to them.[32] The process of Christian self-identification with the Roman 'thing' (later sometimes called *Romania*) had begun even before Constantine, albeit with hesitation and much ambiguity; a hundred years later, the Christian adjustment to political power, to the social structure and the culture of the Roman world, was almost complete.

This wholesale Christianisation of Roman society after Constantine brought the sense of the Church's identity in the secular world under threat. While Christians were an eccentric minority suspect to outsiders and liable to sporadic persecution, their identity in the world had been amply clear. The lines which marked them off from their world were imposed on them by their sheer foreignness to the world. But as Christians became fully assimilated and eventually a dominant majority, as the profession of Christianity became a passport to respectability and privilege, so the lines of demarcation gradually melted away. As Christians ceased to be, visibly, aliens in their world, so the sense of Christian identity inevitably came to be blurred.[33]

Few modern theologians have attached as profound a significance to this upheaval as John Howard Yoder. The transformation of the Church between

---

32. Orosius, *Adv. pag.* 7.41.

33. I have referred to the decades around AD 400, the time when this assimilation of Christianity to Roman society came to its climax, as a 'crisis of identity' for Roman Christians. Robert A. Markus, *The End of Ancient Christianity* (Cambridge, 1990), chap. 1. Much of my argument here is more fully substantiated in that book and is also touched on in Robert A. Markus, 'Church Reform and Society in Late Antiquity' (paper presented at the conference *Ecclesia semper reformanda*, New York, August 2002).

the third and the fifth centuries amounted, in Yoder's eyes, to apostasy. The 'loss of awareness of minority status, transformed into an attitude of "establishment"'—by which, of course, he meant far more than the kind of legal standing enjoyed by the Church of England—'helped let the church cease to be the church'.[34] By accepting its 'establishment' status, the Church had forsaken its calling.[35] Yoder's 'Constantinian heresy' or 'Constantinianism' was the great betrayal of what he called the 'original revolution'. That original revolution was the world-transforming event in which Jesus called his followers around Him into a unique society, founding 'a distinct community with its own deviant set of values and its coherent way of incarnating them'.[36] This, as Yoder saw it, was forsaken under 'Constantinianism': 'The conception of Christianity which took shape between the Edict of Milan and the *City of God* . . . the identification of church and world in . . . mutual approval and support. . . . The church is no longer the obedient suffering line of the true prophets; she has a vested interest in the present order of things and uses the cultic means at her disposal to legitimize that order. She does not preach ethics, judgement, repentance, separation from the world; she dispenses sacraments and holds society together.'[37] Hence, Yoder's repudiation of all the various ways in which the Church has historically been allied to power: 'Should we not rather call into question the tendency—or shall we call it a temptation—of the church to establish symbiotic relations with every social order rather than be critical only of the tactics of having chosen the wrong partner at the wrong time?'[38]

This radical evangelical view rules out from the start any possibility of an area which a shared, secular social or individual morality might inhabit. A moral treatise such as the *Sentences of Sextus*, a work non-Christian in origin but adapted for Christian purposes, or Ambrose's recycling of Cicero's *De officiis*, either would be impossible or would amount to a betrayal of Christian moral teaching. On this view, there can be no moral basis for a

---

34. Yoder, *Original Revolution*, 129; cf. Yoder, *Priestly Kingdom*, 85, 105–8.

35. Yoder, *Original Revolution*, 15.

36. Yoder, *Original Revolution*, 28–29, 35.

37. Yoder, *Original Revolution*, 69 ff. I shall, of course, have to question Yoder's incidental observation, uncritically assumed rather than formulated and established by himself, that 'it is not at all surprising that Augustine, for whom the Constantinian church was a matter of course, should have held that the Roman church was the millennium' (69). For further elaboration of Yoder's idea of modern Constantinianism, and for his various neo-Constantinianisms, see 150–59. See also Yoder, *Priestly Kingdom*, 105–22.

38. Yoder, *Original Revolution*, 157.

secular society. All Yoder's work on Christian social ethics, his repudiation of violence, his radical understanding of Jesus's moral teaching, his insistence that the Christian role in society was that of a 'revolutionary subordination, of willing servanthood in the place of domination',[39] is an exploration of what was implied in this notion of the 'original revolution' and its betrayal by Constantinianism in its various versions.

When Christianity becomes 'established', recognised as the religion of the whole society, membership of the church is in effect identical with membership of the society. One is incorporated in both at once, by birth and (infant) baptism, not by an act of conscious and deliberate decision, a conversion. Christians are no longer made but born.[40] The moral norms for Christian behaviour must now be identical with the norms of the society. Christian norms are to be imposed on all, but at the price of being adapted to be suited for all: 'Since the distinction between church and world is largely lost, the "responsible" church will try to preach a kind of ethics which will work for non-Christians as well as for Christians'.[41] In such a society, the Christian Roman Empire and its successor, medieval (and later) Christendom, the Kingdom is 'in the process of realization through the present order' and the state becomes God's agent in defeating evil.[42] But these are the fruits of the Church's desertion of its vocation by accepting its 'Constantinian' status. Hope of renewal lies only in shaking these foundations, recovering something of the 'logic of its minority stance'.[43]

---

39. Yoder, *Politics of Jesus*, 190.

40. Alan Kreider, 'Changing Patterns of Conversion in the West', in *The Origins of Christendom in the West*, ed. Alan Kreider (Edinburgh, 2001): 'In the early centuries of the church . . . conversion entailed a process of "resocialization" which taught converts the skills and understanding necessary to live the deviant life of an alternative society; and this required of every candidate a "change of life". Now, after Constantine, the alternative society was becoming society itself' (24).

41. Yoder, *Original Revolution*, 82. Interestingly, however, Yoder did soften this dichotomy when he allowed an overlap, restricting the function of secular power 'to protect the innocent and punish the evildoer' (*Original Revolution*, 63). Cf. chap. 2, n. 21, and chap. 3; quoted and discussed by O'Donovan, *Desire of the Nations*, 151–52.

42. Yoder, *Original Revolution*, 70. In Constantinianism 'the purpose of exterminating, rather than subduing, evil, is shifted from the end-time to the present' (71, cf. 73). I explore this in chap. 4. On the 'eschatological gap', see p. 15 above.

43. Yoder, *Original Revolution*, 129; cf. Yoder, *Priestly Kingdom*, 82–87, 121–22. In *Politics of Jesus* Yoder rejected the dichotomy of 'political' versus 'sectarian' as false (110–13), but it is hard to see how 'the creation of an alternative social group', i.e., the Church, can

There are many facets to the Church's loss of its minority stance and its obverse, the process of absorbing and coming to dominate the secular Roman world, and many of them have been amply explored: the Church's relations with political power, its bearers and its exercise; literary and artistic culture; the conventions of public and private life; cults, rituals and celebrations, festivals and observances. The list could be almost endless. In every sphere of life the locus of the line which divided the sacred from the secular was far from fixed, being instead subject to fluctuation, pressures from every side, and constant renegotiation.[44] In all areas, what was at stake were questions such as: How much of what had previously been 'pagan', not of Christian origin, could be shared by Christians with their non-Christian neighbours? What in currently established customs and practises had to be abandoned by a convert to Christianity or renounced by a more than nominally conforming Christian?

These were difficult questions, and the Church's tradition furnished complex, confusing, and uncertain indications of approaches to answering them in the new situation. The Church was spiritually not well prepared for the miracle which had turned it from a persecuted minority into a triumphant majority. In the pre-Constantinian world it had not needed to define its identity, and it now had no ready resources at hand for doing so. The difficulties of drawing clear lines around it have often been insufficiently appreciated. In my book *The End of Ancient Christianity* I urged that the historian of Christianity be sensitive to uncertainty, conscious that the lines between the sacred, the secular, and the profane may be hard to trace and will rarely stay still. 'We may not assume that these boundaries are fixed or constant, that churchmen in Northern Gaul in the sixth century drew them in

---

escape being the 'sect' type, even though it be politically engaged. Cf. Archbishop Rowan Williams's statement that Christianity is 'fundamentally disruptive of pre-existing forms of religious meaning and social belonging. It dissolves earlier worlds of symbolic understanding.' Rowan Williams, 'Defining Heresy', in Kreider, *Origins of Christendom*, 323.

44. I don't know of anything like a comprehensive survey. Some references will be found in Markus, *End of Ancient Christianity*, passim, which is very largely concerned with the Christian response to this process. Johannes Geffcken, *The Last Days of Greco-Roman Paganism*, trans. Sabine MacCormack (Amsterdam, 1978), is perhaps the nearest. See also the classic work of Charles N. Cochrane, *Christianity and Classical Culture* (Oxford, 1957), and, most recently, Hervé Inglebert, *Interpretatio Christiana: Les mutations des savoirs (cosmographie, géographie, ethnographie, histoire) dans l'antiquité chrétienne*, Collection des Études Augustiniennes, Série Antiquité 166 (Paris, 2001).

the same place as would have their colleagues in Italy, their lay congrega-
tions, or their predecessors in the fourth century; still less where a modern
Western scholar might locate them.'[45] In my final chapter I argue that the
decades around AD 400 were a time of particular uncertainty in this respect
and that the period to around 600 was a crucial divide; and I consider the
kind of pressures responsible for shifting its locus. But before that, in my
next two chapters, I turn to Augustine of Hippo, one of the few Christian
writers in Late Antiquity to articulate a response to these uncertainties.

ADDITIONAL NOTE ON SECULAR POWERS

The important and influential discussion of the 'subjection of the nations'
by Oliver O'Donovan in *The Desire of the Nations* (146–57) subtly under-
mines the continuing legitimacy of the secular powers. Commenting on the
verse 'He disarmed the principalities and powers and made a public show of
them in Christ's triumphal procession' (Col. 2:15, in O'Donovan's translation), O'Donovan writes that 'within the framework of these two assertions
there opens up an account of secular authority which presumes neither that
the Christ-event never occurred nor that the sovereignty of Christ is now
transparent and uncontested' (146; italics mine). To be sure, the New Testament leaves us in no doubt that Christ's coming occurred and established
His triumph over the powers. But O'Donovan's last phrase raises a crucial
question concerning the 'transparency' of Christ's sovereignty. He invites us
to imagine Christ's victory as having eradicated, done away with, the reality
of the powers, in terms of an image which suggests that they only *appear*
visible now and that the reality of their obliteration will become apparent
only when Christ's victory is finally revealed. The Pauline eschatology seems,
however, rather to affirm that their authority really does continue and will
do so until the advent of the eschatological Kingdom, without thereby necessarily contesting Christ's victory—and hence authority over them. They
really, and not in mere appearance, continue to be active under the domin-
ion of Christ and will be abrogated only at the establishment of the eschatological Kingdom. They are able to 'contest' Christ's sovereignty only because
they have been allowed to survive, albeit in subjection.

It is important to stress that the contrast between the present *aiôn* and
the *aiôn* to come is not between the appearance and the reality of either

45. Markus, *End of Ancient Christianity*, 9 and passim.

Christ's authority or that of the secular powers. If it were, it would fail to explain the continuing legitimacy of secular powers affirmed in Romans 13. The point about the continuing sway of the powers (Rom. 13:6, above) is not that their remaining authority is mere *appearance*, masked by the present opacity of Christ's victory, to be unmasked as illusory when Christ's triumph over them becomes 'transparent'. It is true that the powers need not necessarily 'contest' Christ's victory. They will, of course, not be in a position to do so when that is finally consummated in the eschatological Kingdom, but for the present they can either rebel or minister to it. What is unmasked as illusion is the appearance of their autonomy, of an independent, absolute sway over us.

In his next paragraph O'Donovan asks, 'To what extent is secular authority compatible with this [the Church's] mission and, so to speak, reauthorised by it?' he answers his question: 'If the mission of the church needs a certain social space, for men and women of every nation to be drawn into the general governed community of God's Kingdom, then secular authority is authorised to provide and ensure that space' (146). Like O'Donovan, I would grant the condition expressed in that 'if', and I accept his conclusion; but I would not restrict the reconceived authority of secular government to securing 'the needs of international mobility and contact which the advancement of the Gospel requires' (147). Paul upholds a more fundamental survival of secular authority, which O'Donovan seems to subvert when he writes that 'no respect can be paid to the role of government, then, as a focus of collective identity, either in Israel or in any other community' (148). I would, on the contrary, wish to read Paul as allowing subordinate identities and loyalties to survive intact under Christ's rule, with their appropriate institutions, norms, and legitimate scope. Thus the contrast that O'Donovan draws between the norms of justice acknowledged within the Christian community and those current outside it is perfectly correct, but the conclusion that 'by embracing the final judgment of God Christians have accepted that they have no need for penultimate judgments to defend their rights' (151) is problematic. Though the statement is true, it slides over an important distinction: they may have no need to defend their own rights within their own community, but they may well need recourse to 'penultimate judgments' for the defence of their rights against outsiders, as, more importantly, will those outsiders for defence of their rights among themselves, and, for that matter, against Christians. The Christian community must acknowledge the need for the secular authorities and their own measures. This need continues to exist in the world around the Christian community.

According to O'Donovan, 'The power that they exercise in defeating their enemies, the national possessions they safeguard, these are now rendered irrelevant by Christ's triumph. This is what might properly be meant by that misleading expression, the "desacralisation" of politics by the Gospel. No government has a right to exist, no nation has a right to defend itself. Such claims are overwhelmed by the immediate claim of the Kingdom' (151). This seems to me to run counter to the more positive Pauline view of the secular powers' continuing and legitimate authority.

ADDITIONAL NOTE ON CHURCH AND SECT

Set in the pagan world, the culture and norms of the Christian group had at first been, necessarily, radical, of the character that Ernst Troeltsch would call the 'sect-type'. All this was to be fundamentally changed in the post-Constantinian world. Unlike many later writers, Troeltsch was acutely conscious of the conceptual problems involved in applying the contrast between 'sect' and 'Church' in the period before the development of an ecclesiastical hierarchy and a sacramental system, not fully realised until the Gregorian reform in the eleventh century; and he had serious reservations about it. The 'sect-type' would finally come into its own and become clearly visible only when its contrast, the 'church-type', made its appearance, with the appearance of the 'established' and dominant majority Church of the Christian Empire of Late Antiquity and the Middle Ages. The 'sectarian' character of pre-Constantinian Christianity gave way to the triumphant Christianity of a universal Church seeking to shape the Christian society around it, to mould its culture and influence the powers that controlled it.[46]

46. Ernst Troeltsch, *The Social Teaching of the Christian Churches,* trans. Olive Wyon (1931), 1:161–64 (on the premedieval church); 328–30 (on medieval sect movements); 331–49 (on the 'sect-type'). It is not necessary here to discuss more recent notions of 'sect'. See, for instance, Roland Robertson, *The Sociological Interpretation of Religion* (Oxford, 1970), or the works of Bryan Wilson and David Martin among many others. A helpful discussion of the terminology is to be found in John Howard Yoder, *The Priestly Kingdom: Social Ethics as Gospel* (Notre Dame, 1984), 197.

2

AUGUSTINE AND THE
SECULARISATION OF ROME

During one of his many journeys between Carthage and his own see of Hippo, in the summer of 404 Augustine was the visiting preacher in a small town in North Africa.[1] Pagans were present in the congregation to hear him. He treated them to a reminder of the Church's triumph in the Roman world: now the persecutors of Christians were conquered—'the Church grew from its own blood, the persecutors have been overcome, the victims of persecution have triumphed' (par. 24, pp. 264–65). 'The promises and prophecies of the Scriptures are being fulfilled, it is wonderful; let them sit up and note the marvellous things that are happening before their eyes, the whole human race streaming together to honour the Crucified. Let the few who have so far remained aloof hear the *strepitus mundi,* the world's roar acclaiming the victory of Christianity' (par. 25, pp. 265–66).

Such celebration of the Christian triumph was not uncommon in Augustine's preaching and writing in the late 390s and the early 400s. Augustine was not alone. The edict *Cunctos populos*[2] ('It is our will that all peoples

---

1. On date and circumstances, see the note to *Sermo Dolbeau* 25 (Mainz 61) in François Dolbeau, ed., *Augustin d'Hippone: Vingt-six sermons au peuple d'Afrique,* Collection des Études Augustiniennes, Série Antiquité 147 (Paris, 1996), 56–57. Further citations to this work are given parenthetically in the text by paragraph number and page number.
2. *CTh* 16.1.2; *CJ* 1.1.1.

ruled by our government shall practice that religion') issued by Theodosius I and his imperial colleagues in 380 was emblematic: the religious legislation gained momentum in the 390s. In Augustine's Africa the climax came in 399 with the arrival of imperial officials in Carthage to destroy the temples and break up the idols.[3] The generation of Romans that had reached adulthood in these decades could not easily escape a sense that they were witnessing a momentous turning point in the history of Christianity as well as of the Roman Empire. These were the 'Christian times', the time of the abandonment of the old gods and the turning of the Roman world to Christianity. Their response to what was happening was neither simple nor uniform.

Most Christians shared the euphoria expressed in Augustine's sermon. Bishops like Ambrose of Milan thought they could discern the signs of the times in the flow of events; they saw the new order of Christianity superseding the ancient Roman traditions, the *mos maiorum*. They were not all as impatient or as energetic in the pursuit of their aims as Ambrose, but they saw themselves as participants in a transformation of the Roman into a Christian world and were impatient for its completion. Their view of the Christian Empire was widely held among preachers and writers and was shared, we must suspect, by the majority of Christians. A new world was taking shape around them and faced them with the necessity of adjusting themselves to their new condition. A great deal in the Church's development in the fourth century can be understood only within the context of an identity crisis brought on by the Church's readiness to assimilate the social order and the culture of the Roman world. In my book *The End of Ancient Christianity* I tried to indicate how late Roman Christians sought to allay their anxieties over the gulf that seemed to have opened between the triumphant Church of the post-Constantinian Empire and its predecessor, the Church of the martyrs. The great need felt by Christians of the post-Constantinian age was for restoration of a lost continuity with the age of persecutions. It was met by three developments: a huge extension of the cult of martyrs, a new interest in the Church's past, and, especially, the growing appeal of asceticism. These were the principal means which helped the Christian community to convince itself that it was still identical with the Church of the martyrs.

---

3. Augustine, *De civ. Dei* 18.54: 'templa everterunt et simulacra fregerunt'. This is the only dated historical report Augustine gives in *De civ. Dei.*

It is important not to mistake these devices of self-reassurance for rejection of, or protest against, the novelty of the Church's recent establishment. Protest and rejection were confined to dissident sects on the fringes of Catholic orthodoxy, which were not recognised by the imperial authorities and were sometimes actively repressed by them. Such dissenting groups found it easier to claim the legacy of the persecuted Church in the new Christian Empire; they preserved their sect status in the new order of things. For the Catholic Church, recovering its links with the past was a far harder task: it had to annex its past from more plausible claimants such as the Donatists and to create the necessary means for doing so. A great deal of effort—spiritual, intellectual, liturgical—was invested in the task of reassuring itself that the newly privileged Church was still the same as its persecuted progenitor. The cult of the martyrs, the ecclesiastical histories, and the ascetic movement were the Church's chief devices for reconciling itself to living in and with a world which it had assimilated and which it was coming to influence and to dominate. By these means mainstream Catholics sought to reassure themselves that triumph did not have to mean betrayal. Appearances notwithstanding, they still were the Church of the martyrs, heirs of their heroic past, distinct in the world around them if not quite foreign to it.

The general acceptance of the new imperial order did, of course, give rise to a variety of anxieties, especially in times of tension and conflict with the imperial 'establishment', and Christians' wholesale assimilation of pagan Roman culture and lifestyles brought unease and opposition (to which I shall return briefly) in some quarters. Except, however, in dissenting groups on the edges of Catholic orthodoxy, the general dispensation of a Church favoured by the powers, recognised by legislation, and sharing Roman lifestyles and culture went unquestioned. Even Augustine was swept off his feet by the prevailing mood of triumphant euphoria.

But only for a few, short years. My view that his jubilant endorsement of the *tempora christiana* was short-lived has not gone unchallenged, and it needs revising in the light of the criticism it has received, but I continue to think it substantially correct.[4] In the years just before and after AD 400

---

4. Robert A. Markus, *Saeculum: History and Society in the Theology of Saint Augustine* (Cambridge, 1970, 2nd ed., 1988). All citations are to the second edition. The argument of my chap. 2 has been called into question by Goulven Madec's '"Tempora Christiana": Expression du triomphalisme chrétien ou récrimination païenne?' in *Scientia Augustiniana: Studien über Augustinus, den Augustinismus und den Augustinerorden*.

Augustine's voice had come to be merged in the 'world's roar' acclaiming Christ's victory (that he had spoken of in the sermon I quoted at the beginning). In these few years he is often celebrating the fulfilment of the prophecies now, very speedily *(valde velociter),*[5] in our time, in these 'Christian times', when God is calling the kings of the earth to His service; the idols have been, or are being, uprooted and the nations gathered from the ends of the earth to the worship of Christ. 'The whole world has become a chorus praising Christ.'[6] But within a few years of preaching to the people of the little town of Boseth, Augustine's enthusiasm abated. One reason for the cooling of his enthusiasm about the 'establishment' of Christianity under the regime of Theodosius and his successors may have been of a practical kind. He had been made aware in his daily dealings with officials that bishops often had little clout and that the influence they could wield on the conduct of affairs was severely limited. The dominance of Christianity in Roman society had in practice not been fully achieved by any means. Bishops could not always count on getting their way; they had to reckon with a deeply entrenched tradition of resistance, often by officials who were still pagan in their allegiance.[7]

The paganism that he encountered in his dealings with officials would not, however, have been the sole reason for Augustine's diminished enthusiasm for the Theodosian establishment. By the year 413 he had embarked on

---

Festschrift Adolar Zumkeller, ed. Cornelius Petrus Mayer and Willigis Eckermann (Würzburg, 1975), 112–36. For my reply and revision in the light of Madec's critique, see Robert A. Markus, '*Tempora Christiana* Revisited', in *Augustine and His Critics: Essays in Honour of Gerald Bonner,* ed. Robert Dodaro and George Lawless (London, 1999), 201–13. Madec does, however, concede that in some of the passages concerned 'on pourrait, à la rigueur, soupçonner quelque accent triomphaliste' (133).

5. Augustine, *Enarr. in Ps.* 6.13.

6. Augustine, *De cons. ev.* 1.32.50–34.52; 26.40; *Enarr. in Ps.* 32.3.9; 149.7; 62.1; *Sermo* 22.4; 328.5.5; *C. Faust.* 13.7, 9; 22.76; *De vera rel.* 3.5. In reference to outlawing of heretics: *Enarr. in Ps.* 59.2 (*ecce nunc*).

7. See, among many studies, Claude Lepelley, 'L'aristocratie lettrée païenne: Une menace aux yeux d'Augustin', in *Augustin prédicateur (395–411),* Actes du Colloque International de Chantilly (5–7 Septembre, 1996), ed. Goulven Madec, Collection des Études Augustiniennes, Série Antiquité 159 (Paris, 1998), 327–42; Claude Lepelley, *Les cités de l'Afrique romaine au Bas-Empire* (Paris, 1979), passim; and *L'évêque dans la cité du IVᵉ au Vᵉ siècle: Image et autorité,* ed. Éric Rebillard and Claire Sotinel, Collection de l'École française de Rome 248 (Rome, 1998), esp. the papers by Rita Lizzi, Éric Rebillard, and Claire Sotinel.

writing the *City of God,* in which he came to formulate the one sustained critique of the prevailing 'dominant narrative'[8] of the Empire's Christianisation. In that great work of his old age Augustine took stock of this narrative as it had come to be constructed by pagans and by Christians respectively: a narrative of failure as seen from the one side, of triumph as seen from the other.

It is the Christian narrative we are concerned with here. In Augustine's time this had firmly settled into its mould shaped by a variety of traditions of discourse. The most fundamental to Augustine's, as indeed to any Christian, understanding of history was the New Testament's time scheme. I have studied Augustine's account of sacred and secular history at tedious length in my *Saeculum* and can be brief here. Christians had always known that with the coming of Christ the world entered a new age. The prophets and the biblical writers had singled out one strand in the world's history, the narrative of Israel, culminating in the story of Jesus. In Him the promise and the prophecies were fulfilled. The Christian Church was henceforth the new chosen people until the final return of the Saviour to gather His faithful into His Kingdom. This stretch of time, the 'sixth age' as they reckoned it, between Incarnation and *parousia* was of unknown duration (Augustine was among those most insistent on this); its content and its direction were unpredictable. We have no divinely authorised prophets or evangelists to interpret for us in the perspective of the history of salvation the significance of events in this last, the sixth, age—none to single out an identifiable strand as part of our salvation history. God was, of course, active in all history, as He had been outside the particular and narrow strand of narrative which constituted the salvation history between Creation and Incarnation; of course, He would continue to act in all history, and nothing would be remote from His providence. But nowhere outside the Bible could the Church be bound to an authoritative insight into the meaning of any historical event or process in the scheme of salvation. God's purposes might occasionally be disclosed to some later prophet *quasi privatim,* as Augustine would say,[9] 'personally'; but the revelation of His purposes in the public history of salvation was closed. In the sacred history the rest of this 'last age' is a blank.

---

8. I borrow the phrase and some of the argument from Peter Brown's *Authority and the Sacred: Aspects of the Christianisation of the Roman World* (Cambridge, 1995), esp. its first chapter.

9. Augustine, *De vera rel.* 25.46.

These immense simplicities of their faith were, however, confused for Christians by the momentous events of the fourth century. The miraculous triumph of their religion had somehow come to subvert the sense of the homogeneity of this 'sixth age'. Eusebius had come close to speaking of Constantine in messianic terms, clothing the emperor's conversion with a significance in the sacred history: it became a landmark to divide these last times. The era inaugurated by Constantine, followed within two generations by the official imposition of Christian orthodoxy on the Empire, was greeted by euphoric Christians as the time of the fulfilment of ancient prophecies. Pagans, too, were conscious of a new era: for them, a time of foreboding and disaster. These were the 'Christian times' *(tempora christiana)*. In the confrontation of pagan with Christian in the decades around 400 this slice of history became the subject of polemic and indeed gained sharper definition (notably in the polemic of Augustine's *City of God*) in consequence.

Augustine had, like everyone else, come under the spell of the exhilaration over Christian triumph and, as we have seen, echoed the general sentiments of his contemporaries. In some of his earlier works, the contemporary history of Christianisation and victory over paganism had been drawn into the framework of the sacred history. But all this was reversed in his *City of God*. This work was an uncompromising rejection of any claim to knowing the duration of this last age or the direction of its future course. Between the Incarnation and the *parousia* history was, in Augustine's final view, totally 'secular', containing no signposts to sacred meaning, no landmarks in the history of salvation. In terms of their ultimate significance, in relation to salvation or damnation, history remained opaque to human scrutiny: 'In this world the two Cities are inextricably intertwined and mingled with each other, until they shall be separated in the last judgement'.[10] The bond that linked the Roman Empire and Christianity was now a contingent historical fact, which might at any future time be dissolved, even reversed. The Empire

---

10. Augustine, *De civ. Dei* 1.35. Cf. Markus, *Saeculum*, chap. 3. Henri-Irénée Marrou comments on this in his *Théologie de l'histoire* (Paris, 1968): 'Toute action historique nous est apparue comme pouvant s'analyser ou plutôt se décomposer entre l'une et l'autre, comme dans l'électrolyse se séparent les ions,—étant toujours bien entendu qu'une telle analyse ou décompostition n'est effectivement concevable que dans l'eschatologie ou pour la pensée divine' (129).

had no specially privileged place in God's providence either as an instrument of or as an obstacle to the achievement of His purposes. There was nothing intrinsically sacred about it; it was a *res publica*[11] among others.

The contrast with the dominant Christian narrative could hardly be sharper.[12] Rufinus, for instance, from whose appendix to Eusebius's *Ecclesiastical History* Augustine had learned most of what he knew about the post-Constantinian Church, had presented his narrative within a framework of the victory of Christianity over *superstitio* and idolatry; the story was a record of *mirabilia dei*.[13] Augustine's radical agnosticism about God's purposes in human history undermined all such certainties. There could be no assurance of conclusive victory; the Theodosian achievement stood under a final question mark. The workings of God in the future, as in the present, remained inscrutable.

Augustine's mature reflection has been said 'to protect the merciful opacity of human affairs. In declaring the *saeculum* to be largely opaque to human scrutiny, Augustine protected the richness of human culture from the hubris of those who wanted to relate every aspect of the world around them directly to the sacred.'[14] To assert the autonomy of the secular was to resist any hostile takeover of this middle ground between sacred and profane from either side: either to include it in the sacred—by Christian or by pagan—or to repudiate it as irredeemably profane or demonic. Augustine's views on these subjects had grown from a need to evaluate in a Christian perspective a whole cultural and political tradition which had been the vehicle of pagan religious values. Already in the mid-390s, as a young bishop, Augustine had struggled in his *De doctrina Christiana* to define the value

11. When speaking of Augustine, I keep the Latin phrase in preference over its antiquated though accurate equivalent, 'commonwealth'; in the context of modern political thought I shall use the phrase 'civil community'.

12. The contrast with Orosius has been much studied, notably by Theodor E. Mommsen; for references, see Markus, *Saeculum*, 31, 54, 161–64.

13. Françoise Thélamon, *Païens et chrétiens au IVe siècle: L'apport de l'«Histoire ecclésiastique» de Rufin d'Aquilée* (Paris, 1981), 468–70 and passim. She describes Rufinus's history as 'a sacred history' *(une histoire sainte)*: it aims to show 'how God's design for the world manifests itself in events' (26, 159). I have considered such views in more detail in Robert A. Markus, 'L'autorité épiscopale et la définition de la chrétienté', *Studia Ephemeridis Augustinianum* 58 (1997): 37–43.

14. Peter Brown, 'Introducing Robert Markus', *Augustinian Studies* 32 (2001): 184. I return to this theme in chap. 4.

of the secular disciplines. He could not accept that they were indissolubly linked (as the emperor Julian, among other late-fourth-century pagans, wished to claim) to pagan religion and were thus, from a Christian point of view, to be rejected. Many Christians had clung to them, sometimes without anxiety, sometimes despite acknowledged but unresolved tension. In his *De doctrina Christiana* Augustine had made the case for the legitimacy, indeed the necessity, of adopting the secular disciplines—that is, the established components of the syllabus of current Roman education—for the purposes of a Christian education, in subordination to and integrated into a study of Christian wisdom, based on a scriptural foundation, carried out in faith.[15] This was a particular case of his more general distinction—also stated in that same work—that among human institutions only those that are essentially linked to demonic practices are to be rejected (these we may call the profane); of the rest, some may be superfluous and extravagant, others convenient and necessary for human purposes and of value when utilised within a life ordered by love of God.[16] In Augustine's classification of human institutions these come close to what I think of as the secular. Augustine's trichotomy could well be reckoned as the charter for what Charles Taylor has labelled, after the Jesuit missionary in China, the 'Ricci project': the project of adapting Christianity to an alien culture 'involves the difficult task of making new discriminations: what in the culture represents a valid human difference, and what is incompatible with Christian faith?'[17]

In the *City of God* Augustine's perspective was wider, but an analogous model enabled him to concede value to social structures and cultural forms of non-Christian origin. Among the tangled roots of that 'great and arduous work'[18] was the need Augustine felt to show, both to Christians and to their non-Christian fellows, that Christians had a stake in the Roman *res publica*. That was the overriding concern in his correspondence with the pagan

---

15. This is, of course, the theme of Henri-Irénée Marrou's great work *Saint Augustin et la fin de la culture antique* (Paris, 1938; reprinted with his *Retractatio,* 1949). On the background to this, see Robert A. Markus, 'Paganism, Christianity and the Latin Classics', in *Fourth Century Latin Literature,* ed. J. W. Binns, Studies in Latin Literature (London, 1974), 1–21; reprinted in Robert A. Markus, *From Augustine to Gregory the Great: History and Christianity in Late Antiquity* (London, 1983), article V.

16. Augustine, *De doctr. Christ.* 2.25.38.

17. Charles Taylor, 'A Catholic Modernity?' in *A Catholic Modernity? Charles Taylor's Marianist Award Lecture,* ed. James L. Heft (New York, 1999), 16.

18. 'Magnum opus et arduum': from Augustine, *De civ. Dei, Praef.*

aristocrat Volusianus and the Christian official Marcellinus at the moment when he was setting out on the great project of the *City of God*. In this interchange we can observe the creation of a shared space in which both the bishop, on the one side, and the civil official, on the other, are allowed the freedom to act on their own proper principles—a space that is at the same time a territory in which each of the two parties can allow the other to occupy its own distinct and proper position. This is the emergence of the secular in action.[19] In the course of writing the work Augustine would need to define the intermediate place in which was situated the *res publica*, somewhere between two extremes: on the one side, the sacredness claimed for it by the Christian rhetoric of Empire in a tradition of Eusebius (still highly visible in his own day, shaping, for instance, the poetry of Prudentius or the histories of Rufinus and Orosius), as well as by the pretensions to a sacred destiny given it in the ancient Virgilian literary tradition that still held educated imaginations in its grip; and, on the other side, a refusal to acknowledge a legitimate concern for the destinies of *Romania* or a dismissal of its claims on Christian loyalties. As in the *De doctrina Christiana*, here again Augustine wanted to establish a sphere in which pagan and Christian both had a stake. This was the *saeculum*—not a third City between the earthly and the heavenly, but their mixed, 'inextricably intertwined' state in this temporal life.[20]

From the beginning, Augustine's objective was to define a civil community in a way which would enable Christians to give full weight to its claims on them, no less than on its pagan citizens and functionaries, while at the same time deflating the more grandiose, quasi-divine, claims made for it, either by pagans or by Christians. The long and winding argumentation of *The City of God* brought Augustine in Book 19 to 'place' this social and political entity in its proper relation to the heavenly City. Well known though

19. The correspondence has been discussed in detail by Robert Dodaro in several papers, esp. 'Augustine of Hippo between the Secular City and the City of God' (paper presented at the Atelier sur les frontiéres du profane dans l'Empire romain pendant l'Antiquité tardive, École française de Rome, Rome, 23–24 April 2004). I have also touched on the theme in Robert A. Markus, '*De ciuitate dei*: Pride and the Common Good', in *Augustine: 'Second Founder of the Faith'*, ed. Joseph C. Schnaubelt and Frederick Van Fleteren, Collectanea Augustiniana (New York, 1990), 245–59; reprinted in Robert A. Markus, *Sacred and Secular: Studies on Augustine and Latin Christianity* (London, 1994), article III.

20. See Markus, *Saeculum*, 62–71, and Henri-Irénée Marrou, 'Civitas Dei, civitas terrena: Num tertium quid?' *Studia Patristica* 2 (1957): 342–50.

they are, it is as well to quote the crucial paragraphs of Augustine's statement:[21]

> The heavenly City, while on its earthly pilgrimage, calls forth its citizens from every nation and every tongue. It assembles a band of pilgrims, not caring about any diversity in customs, laws, and institutions whereby they severally make provision for the achievement and maintenance of earthly peace. All these provisions are intended, in their various ways among the different nations, to secure the aim of earthly peace. The heavenly City does not repeal or abolish any of them, provided that they do not impede the religion in which the one supreme and true God is taught to be worshipped.
>
> So the heavenly City, too, uses the earthly peace in the course of its earthly pilgrimage. It cherishes and fosters, as far as it can without compromising its faith and devotion, the orderly coherence of men's wills concerning the things which pertain to the mortal nature of man; and this earthly peace it directs to the attainment of heavenly peace.

Political institutions, social practices, customs—are all radically relativized. In so restricting their sphere, Augustine is at the same time asserting their autonomy within their restricted sphere. In a Christian perspective, they are neutral; they can be used rightly, directed to the enjoyment of eternal peace by members of the heavenly City, or wrongly, directed to the enjoyment of lesser goods, the earthly peace.[22] In the most general terms, for Augustine political discourse is concerned, not with the ultimate realities of human fulfilment and salvation, but with what, in Dietrich Bonhoeffer's language, we might call the 'penultimate'.[23]

A well-brought-up and properly modest historian might be wise to stop at this point. My conclusion that in the *City of God* Augustine took the measure of the Roman past in relation to his vision of history and deflated its pretensions to a sacred destiny—sacred in both the pagan and the Christian viewpoints—while, at the same time, vindicating its secular role is not now

---

21. Augustine, *De civ. Dei* 19.17. Cf. Markus, *Saeculum*, 70–71.

22. Augustine, *De civ. Dei* 19.14. I return to a fuller discussion of this in chap. 3.

23. Bonhoeffer's 'penultimate' invites comparison with the 'infravalent ends' of Jacques Maritain, e.g., in his *True Humanism*, trans. M. R. Anderson (London, 1946), 143–44.

likely to be very controversial.[24] If, however, we ask about the implications of Augustine's views, we enter deeper waters and controversy. Although much has been written about Augustine's 'political thought', it would be generally agreed that he had little interest in anything we might call by that name. Nevertheless, when dealing with a thinker of his stature, it is hardly satisfactory to stop here. For anyone who has spent much time in the close presence of Augustine's writings, it is very hard to treat his text in its frozen fixity, without engaging in the kind of problems that concerned him. Almost inevitably, the reader is drawn into a dialogue of some kind with Augustine— a dialogue that will also be a conversation with one's own past self, with colleagues and teachers of one's own and earlier generations; and one that is likely to continue with every reading and rereading of Augustine's text. Much of Western theology as well as of political thought has in fact been, at least in part, such a long-drawn-out conversation. It is one from which I cannot, as a modern Western European, stand aside. The questions which exercised Augustine are the great fundamental questions about human social existence. He has something to say to us, no less than to his contemporaries. To understand what he is saying to us, we need to listen carefully to what he says to them, but we cannot stop there.

Broadly speaking, two types of social thought have claimed the authority of the Augustinian tradition and have claimed to interpret it in modern terms. One is that of the secular liberalism which would seek to sever any direct relation between religion and the public realm. The other is the opposite of this: the tradition which would see the public sphere as founded on or tied in one way or another to Christianity. I shall deal with the first, the 'secularist', interpretation of Augustine in my next chapter. Here I start with the second of these ways of reading Augustine, historically by far the more influential and important way, which held sway during most of the centuries between Augustine's death and at least to early modern times and has been revived in our own days.

At the heart of this way of thinking is the radical equation of the secular with sin. John Milbank, to take a modern example of this venerable tradition of interpreting Augustine, writes:

---

24. Cf. M. J. Hollerich, 'John Milbank, Augustine and the "Secular"', in *History, Apocalypse and the Secular Imagination*, ed. Mark Vessey, Karla Pollmann, and Allan D. Fitzgerald (Bowling Green, OH, 1999), 311–26, esp. the summary statement on 326.

This *civitas* [the *civitas terrena*] as Augustine finds it in the present, is the vestigial remains of an entirely pagan mode of practice, stretching back to Babylon. There is no set of positive objectives that are its own peculiar business, and the City of God makes *usus* of exactly the same range of finite goods, although for different ends, with 'a different faith, a different hope, a different love' [*De civ. Dei* 18.54]. For the ends sought by the *civitas terrena* are not merely limited, finite goods, they are those finite goods regarded without 'referral' to the infinite good, and, in consequence, they are unconditionally *bad* ends. The realm of the merely practical, cut off from the ecclesial, is quite simply a realm of sin.[25]

Although some of the assumptions behind this statement are very open to question, a great deal in Augustine's thought points in this direction.[26] There is certainly a sense in which Augustine was committed to the view that only in the Church, and indeed only in the Church as it will be in its final, eschatologically purified state, can justice properly speaking be realised. The claim that classical political theory is relocated by Christianity as thought about the Church has solid foundations in Augustine's thought: especially in his mature thinking as it developed under the overwhelmingly anti-Pelagian concern that had come to be pervasive in it.[27] This would give some support to the view of the Church as the exemplary community espoused by theologians who like to describe themselves as 'radically orthodox'. According to theologians of this persuasion, 'The fullness of the gospel demands . . . something like a premodern understanding of the integrity of

25. John Milbank, *Theology and Social Theory: Beyond Secular Reason* (Oxford, 1990), 406. Italics as in the original. For the whole argument, see his chapter 'The Other City: Theology as a Social Science'. I comment on this statement below.

26. The most powerful, though also subtly nuanced, statement I know of is the book by Robert Dodaro, *Christ and the Just Society in the Thought of Augustine* (Cambridge, 2004), 112, 183.

27. I admit the justice of criticisms of my minimising unduly in my *Saeculum* the social character of the church, though I would have reservations about John Milbank's view that 'as a civitas, the Church is, for Augustine, itself a "political" reality' (*Theology and Social Theory*, 403). For a more sophisticated form of such criticism, see Rowan Williams, 'Politics and the Soul: A Reading of the *City of God*', *Milltown Studies* 19/20 (1987): 55–72: Augustine 'is engaged in a *redefinition* of the public self, designed to show that it is life outside the Christian community which fails to be truly public, authentically political' (58; italics in original).

the Christian community'[28]—what in common usage would be meant by 'Christendom'. In such a view no sound political theory can be constructed except within the framework of a Christian 'ontology' or worldview.

If true justice is dependent on true piety, as Augustine undoubtedly held, then it is certainly true that Augustine could not envisage any community other than the Church as capable of realising the political objectives of the *res publica*. For if justice *(iustitia)* in the full-blooded sense given it by Augustine is an essential constituent of the notion of 'what is right' *(iuris consensus)*, then evidently 'where there is no true justice there can be no *ius* either',[29] and, as Augustine concludes, *that* true justice 'is found only where the one true God alone rules by grace over a society which obeys Him and sacrifices only to Him, in all of whose members the body is subject to the soul, the vices to reason in observance of the right order; in that city the whole community and people, like the individual just man, live in that faith which works by love, that love whereby man loves God as He is to be loved and his neighbour as he loves himself.'[30] Augustine not only accepts the conclusion but insists on the impossibility of true justice being attained, even by just and pious believers, except by humility, with the help of God's grace.

This holds for true or perfect virtue, virtue which avails a person for salvation. But Augustine's polemic against the virtues of pagans should not induce us to believe that all acts of virtue, to be virtuous, need to be perfectly virtuous, that justice can be real only when perfect. Even though, as he has just told us, true or perfect justice, like the true or perfect virtue which procures salvation, can be possessed only by those who have true *pietas*, he nevertheless leaves no doubt that an imperfect but useful virtue can be found among citizens of the earthly City.[31] The same goes for justice: an imperfect or relative version of justice may be found in all sorts of places,

28. Paul Lakeland, *Postmodernity: Christian Identity in a Fragmented Age* (Minneapolis, 1997), 43. Lakeland describes these views as 'counter-modern Christendom' and nostalgic in character and as 'shameless reassertion of the premodern superiority of Christendom' (68).

29. Augustine, *De civ. Dei* 19.21.1.

30. Augustine, *De civ. Dei* 19.23.5.

31. E.g., Augustine, *De civ. Dei* 5.19. The distinction between *virtus ipsa* and *vera* or *perfecta* has been decisively established, with many further references, by C. Tornau in 'Does Augustine Accept Pagan Virtue?' (paper presented at the 14th International Conference on Patristic Studies in Oxford, 2003). I thank Dr. Tornau for his courtesy in providing me with a text of this paper.

although its full realisation will only be in the eschatologically purified Church. Here on earth justice may be achieved, but it will always be necessarily an imperfect justice. A just society is a penitent society.[32] Being imperfectly just is not the same thing as being unjust.

Conceding Augustine's principle that all that is not of grace is sin, does it necessarily follow, as has been alleged, that there is no 'neutral public sphere in which people can act politically without reference to ultimate ends'?[33] Two separate points need to be cleared up in answering this question. First, it is evident that for Augustine individual persons will necessarily have their own ultimate ends, to which all their actions, in whatever sphere, are referred, and on which their salvation or damnation depends. There is nothing exceptional about a public sphere in this respect. Acting politically is, like acting in any other sphere, never morally indifferent. On Augustinian premises, it is bound to be either sinful or not. If it is not sinful, then it depends for its goodness on grace and all that is involved in the life of grace: 'that faith which', as Augustine put it in the text just quoted,[34] 'works by love'.

The second point raised by the question concerns the 'neutral public sphere'. When we ask whether there is a 'neutral public sphere in which people can act politically without reference to ultimate ends?', the answer, as I have just said, must be no, because people cannot act intentionally in any sphere without reference to ultimate ends. But it is important to note that the implication of this is not that there is no 'neutral public sphere' but that there is no morally indifferent action within it. It is not necessary to think of such a sphere as the sum of a multiplicity or a fabric woven of many actions by many people; indeed, it makes little sense to do so, and I am sure this is not how Augustine thought of it. He seems to have thought of it in much less personal terms, as what we might call practices, customs, institutions. They may be the cumulative effect of long sequences of human action, shaped by collective behaviour over many generations, routinised or institutionalised over time. They have come to form a complex which now helps to shape and condition human action and behaviour, but they determine it no more—and no less—than a language determines what we say in it.

32. Augustine, *De civ. Dei* 19.27. This has been stressed by Dodaro, *Christ and the Just Society*, 153–58.

33. This is the formulation of Milbank's reading of Augustine by Hollerich, 'John Milbank', 315.

34. Augustine, *De civ. Dei* 19.23.5.

In this respect there is a close parallel between the way Augustine treats the constituents of secular culture in the *De doctrina Christiana* and the way he thinks of acting within the framework of existing social and political institutions. Indeed, in that work, Augustine says something to this effect more or less explicitly.[35] As with the curriculum of the established educational system, and, generally, with established practices, customs, and institutions, members of the two Cities make use of the same finite goods, although for different ends, with 'a different faith, a different hope, a different love'.[36] This is the principle which allowed Augustine to deny any sharp break separating the ancient structures and culture of the classical city from the Christianised Roman society of his day. Of course the direct link between *polis* and virtue was now severed. The *polis* could no longer serve as its members' educator in justice and the instrument of perfecting human life; that role was now abrogated, taken over by the Church. But the Church, expressing its social character in its sacramental life, continued to exist within the boundaries of the (ancient) civic community, within the conditions provided by it for its ecclesial life. That secular framework demanded acknowledgement of its function and value, while at the same time it needed to be critically distanced and assessed within a Christian perspective.

From all this I must conclude that any reading of Augustine that denies the legitimacy or value of secular political or social structures and of the established practices of a secular culture in a Christian perspective is a misreading. This conclusion, however, should not be taken to justify the opposite type of claim to Augustinian support, that of a secular liberalism that severs any relation between religion and public authority and upholds an open, pluralistic, and religiously neutral civic community. That claim I consider in my next chapter.

Additional Note on the Morality of Actions, Practices, and Institutions

Augustine, of course, could scarcely be expected to have had the concepts and the language available to him to speak of practices and institutions.

---

35. Augustine, *De doctr. Christ.* 2.25.38.

36. Augustine, *De civ. Dei* 18.54. I consider in chap. 3, on p. 67, the modern analogue of 'overlapping consensus'.

Nevertheless, it is clear that he was thinking in something like these terms. This may seem obvious, but is so often ignored (as it is by John Milbank) that it is necessary to clarify the matter. Even at the cost of belabouring the rather obvious point, we must note that Augustine allows no doubt that citizens of the heavenly City may discharge public functions in the *res publica*:[37] in other words, he assumes that the moral qualities of institutions and those of the actions of individuals within them are to be distinguished. It is absolutely clear that Augustine envisaged a possibility of acting morally, with God's grace, within the framework of earthly political order. Milbank, however, asserts that 'the ends sought by the *civitas terrena* are not merely limited, finite goods, they are those finite goods regarded without "referral" to the infinite good, and, in consequence, they are unconditionally *bad* ends.'[38] The statement is true only if read as referring, not to a 'neutral public sphere in which people can act politically without reference to ultimate ends',[39] but to individual members of the *civitas terrena*, taken strictly in the sense of the *civitas terrena* as the community of the proud and the selfish, those predestined to be damned. But the 'realm of the merely practical' is not identical with the *civitas terrena* understood in this narrow sense (the sense it usually bears when Augustine defines it explicitly—as, for instance, defined by 'love of self in contempt of God', in one of his formulations).[40] If, however, the *civitas terrena* is understood in its wider sense as the mixed society on earth comprising both virtuous and wicked members (for which warrant can easily be found in Augustine)—that is, the 'realm of the practical'—then it includes members of the *civitas Dei*, mixed into the community of the sinful. Plainly, its ends are not only the 'merely limited, finite goods . . . those finite goods regarded without "referral" to the infinite good, and, in consequence, . . . unconditionally *bad* ends'.[41] It follows that it includes, along with these bad ends, 'limited, finite goods' *with* 'referral' to the infinite good, namely, by those members of the *civitas Dei* who are active in the *civitas terrena*. If *civitas terrena* in Milbank's statement refers to the community of the proud and selfish, it tells us nothing about the realm of social

37. See esp. Augustine, *Enarr. in Ps.* 61.8: 'terrena res publica habet cives nostros administrantes res eius'. For more discussion and documentation, see, e.g., Markus, *Saeculum*, 58–60.

38. Milbank, *Theology and Social Theory*, 406.

39. Hollerich, 'John Milbank'.

40. Augustine, *De civ. Dei* 14.28.

41. Milbank, *Theology and Social Theory*, 406.

and political activity; if it stands for the earthly City in its wider sense, it is simply untrue.

If I labour this point it is because it is critically important to be clear that empirical groups, institutions, and societies are, for Augustine, always and necessarily composites of the two Cities, taken in their strict eschatological meaning. A great deal of the confusion and the controversy over the 'secular' realm in Augustine's thought arises from failure to distinguish the two senses that the 'earthly City' can bear in Augustine's language. The 'earthly City', 'Babylon', stands both for the impious City or empire, the symbol of the eschatologically separated, unredeemed community of the reprobate, and any actual, empirical society, in which good Christians may discharge public functions, rubbing shoulders with wicked Christian and pagan fellow-citizens. It is the first sense that Augustine has in mind when he defines the earthly City in moral or theological terms—identified by pride, impiety, love of self, enjoyment of ends lower than God, predestination to damnation. But he also speaks of it in concrete, empirical terms, as exemplified by the Roman Empire or other kingdoms. These latter, like all groups, obviously do contain among their citizens individual members of the City of God. As societies, they cannot be directly assessed in terms of the moral qualities applicable to action and intention. Such norms (self-love vs. love of God, etc.) cannot apply to practices, cultures, institutions, or social structures. Societies, institutions, and practices are incapable of salvation or damnation; they are of an impersonal nature. (They are, however, not morally neutral, as I hope to show in chapter 3, in as much as they can be better or worse according to the kind of activity and intentions they promote and the kind of people they help to shape. Where they differ from individuals is that they have no eschatological destiny, no intentions which can be directed to ultimate ends, good or bad.) The morality of acting in the *saeculum*, within the framework of the established order of things, is determined by human intentionality: in Augustine's language, referred by members of the heavenly City to the enjoyment of eternal peace and to the enjoyment of lesser goods by members of the earthly City.[42] Milbank's statement that 'the

---

42. Augustine, *De civ. Dei* 19.14. Something like the view put forward in this paragraph seems to me to me hinted at by Gaetano Lettieri, *Il senso della storia in Agostino d'Ippona* (Rome, 1988), 300–304. Cf. Miikka Ruokanen, *Theology of Social Life in Augustine's 'De civitate Dei'* (Göttingen, 1993), who writes: 'Augustine accepts that the forms of maintaining concord among men are adiaphora.' (151).

ends sought by the *civitas terrena* are not merely limited, finite goods, they are those finite goods regarded without "referral" to the infinite good, and, in consequence, . . . unconditionally *bad* ends'[43] is true only in so far as it says nothing about the 'public realm' and can be made relevant to it only by obliterating the difference between the eschatological *civitas terrena* (the community of those predestined to damnation) and earthly societies, with their essentially mixed character and the mixture of ends represented in them. This eschatological insistence is the key to Augustine's notion of the *saeculum*—that is, of the realm in which the careers of the two Cities are inextricably intertwined.[44]

43. Milbank, *Theology and Social Theory*, 406.
44. See Markus, *Saeculum*, 62–63 and 102–3.

3

CONSENSUS IN AUGUSTINE AND THE
LIBERAL TRADITION

I concluded my last chapter with the reflection that no interpretation of Augustine that does not allow an important place in his thought for a secular realm can be considered acceptable.[1] This does not in itself justify fathering modern secular liberalism on Augustine. In this chapter I want to consider what kind of a political theory in present-day terms an Augustinian model of society might point to. I want to stress at the outset that this question is not primarily a historical one. It is not about what Augustine himself thought so much as an attempt at a selective retrieval of a tradition, involving a reinterpretation of its elements in a new intellectual situation.

In the chapter of the *City of God* crucial to our purpose Augustine gives some hints concerning the direction that his thoughts on the tasks and responsibilities of the civil community might have taken, had he wanted to develop them. His keynote is consensus: 'The heavenly City during its pilgrimage here on earth makes use of the earthly peace and of a certain cohesion of human wills concerning the things pertaining to men's mortal

---

1. Others who reach this conclusion, by other routes, include Jean B. Elshtain, *Augustine and the Limits of Politics* (Notre Dame, IN, 1998), 98. Cf. also Ernest L. Fortin, *Political Idealism and Christianity in the Thought of St Augustine* (Villanova, PA, 1972): 'There is, strictly speaking, for Augustine no such thing as a Christian polity. Christianity was never intended as a substitute for political life' (32).

nature'.[2] The 'cohesion of human wills'—or the consensus—of which he is speaking here is central to his conception of what the earthly and the heavenly Cities share: he insists on it twice in the same chapter. On both occasions the consensus is confined to 'the things pertaining to our mortal life'.[3] It is tempting to construe these expressions rather narrowly: to define a sphere for the exercise of secular power and to limit its scope to maintaining security, law and order, and the satisfaction of material needs, without regard to moral standards and spiritual values. These functions are certainly part of what Augustine took to be the scope of the public authority; but to confine its scope to them would attribute to him a far more negative view of its importance than he would have intended and, in doing so, would make

2. Augustine, *De civ. Dei* 19.17. In view of its central importance, I quote the text in full: 'utitur ergo etiam caelestis civitas in hac sua peregrinatione pace terrena et de rebus ad mortalem hominum naturam pertinentibus humanarum voluntatum compositionem, quantum salva pietate ac religione conceditur, tuetur atque appetit eamque terrenam pacem refert ad caelestem pacem, quae vere ita pax est, ut rationalis dumtaxat creaturae sola pax habenda atque dicenda sit, ordinatissima scilicet et concordissima societas fruendi deo et invicem in deo; quo cum ventum erit, non erit vita mortalis, sed plane certeque vitalis, nec corpus animale, quod, dum, corrumpitur, adgravat animam, sed spiritale sine ulla indigentia ex omni parte subditum voluntati. Hanc pacem, dum peregrinatur in fide, habet atque ex hac fide iuste vivit, cum ad illam pacem adipiscendam refert quidquid bonarum actionum gerit ergo deum et proximum, quoniam vita civitatis utique socialis est.' The point is also made earlier in the same chapter: 'idcirco rerum vitae huic mortali necessariarum utrisque hominibus et utrique domui communis est usus; sed finis utendi cuique suus proprius multumque diversus. Ita etiam terrena civitas, quae non vivit ex fide, terrenam pacem appetit in eoque defigit imperandi oboediendique concordiam civium, ut sit eis de rebus ad mortalem vitam pertinentibus humanarum quaedam compositio voluntatum. Civitas autem caelestis vel potius pars eius, quae in hac mortalitate peregrinatur et vivit ex fide, etiam ista pace necesse est utatur, donec ipsa, cui talis pax necessaria est, mortalitas transeat; ac per hoc, dum apud terrenam civitatem velut captivam vitam suae peregrinationis agit, iam promissione redemptionis et dono spiritali tamquam pignore accepto legibus terrenae civitatis, quibus haec administrantur, quae sustentandae mortali vitae adcommodata sunt, obtemperare non dubitat, ut, quoniam communis est ipsa mortalitas, vel seruetur in rebus ad eam pertinentibus inter civitatem utramque concordia.'

3. They are spelt out in Augustine, *De civ. Dei* 19.13: 'Deus . . . dedit hominibus quaedam bona huic vitae congrua, id est pacem temporalem pro modulo mortalis vitae in ipsa salute et incolumitate ac societate sui generis, et quaeque huic paci vel tuendae vel recuperandae necessaria sunt (sicut ea, quae apte et conuenienter adiacent sensibus, lux vox, aurae spirabiles aquae potabiles, et quidquid ad alendum tegendum curandum ornandumque corpus congruit).'

him a precursor of modern secular liberalism. My own interpretation of the political implications of Augustine's views has come perilously close to doing this, and I must plead guilty to the charge as stated by one of the most fair-minded and perspicacious of my critics, that my interpretation 'of the secular state seems cast in terms drawn entirely from modern individualist liberalism, in which the state is founded on contract and consent, not on our nature as social beings, and which lacks any transcendental legitimation or attachment.' As this critic goes on to point out, 'Such a state must necessarily be secular, open, pluralistic, religiously neutral—freedom plus groceries, as one admirer has described the goal of the liberal state.'⁴ In good Augustinian fashion, I want to devote the rest of this chapter to a reconsideration—a *retractatio*—of this view.

It is as well to indicate here the features of a secular society as it is understood in the classical liberal tradition. I take the following description from D. L. Munby, *The Idea of a Secular Society*,⁵ written in direct response to T. S. Eliot's lecture 'The Idea of a Christian Society.'⁶ 'A secular society is one which explicitly refuses to commit itself as a whole to any particular view of the nature of the universe and the place of man in it. In particular, it will be neutral as between religious traditions' (14). (b) 'Such a society is unlikely to

---

4. M. J. Hollerich, 'John Milbank, Augustine and the "Secular"', in *History, Apocalypse and the Secular Imagination*, ed. Mark Vessey, Karla Pollmann, and Allan D. Fitzgerald (Bowling Green, OH, 1999), 320. The phrase is attributed to Max Lerner (n. 15). Among the works from which I have learnt most in connection with the theme explored in the rest of this lecture I must single out Oliver O'Donovan's *The Desire of the Nations: Rediscovering the Roots of Political Theology* (Oxford, 1996). Concerning my interpretation of Augustine's revision of the Ciceronian definition of the *res publica* (Robert A. Markus, *Saeculum: History and Society in the Theology of Saint Augustine,* 2nd ed. [Cambridge, 1988], 64–66), see also Oliver O'Donovan, 'Augustine's *City of God* XIX and Western Political Thought', *Dionysius* 11 (1987): 99–100; R. D. Williams, 'Politics and the Soul: A Reading of the *City of God*', *Milltown Studies* 19/20 (1987): 58–60. I should also mention here Gerald Bonner, '*Quid imperatori cum ecclesia?* St Augustine on History and Society', *Augustinian Studies* 2 (1971): 231–51; Miikka Ruokanen, *Theology of Social Life in Augustine's 'De civitate Dei'* (Göttingen, 1993), 151–53; Johannes van Oort, *Jerusalem and Babylon: A Study of Augustine's 'City of God' and the Sources of His Doctrine of the Two Cities* (New York, 1991), 127–29; Elshtain, *Augustine*, 92–101; P. J. Burnell, 'The Status of Politics in St Augustine's *City of God*', *History of Political Thought* 13 (1992): 14–29; and Robert Dodaro, *Christ and the Just Society in the Thought of Augustine* (Cambridge, 2004).

5. D. L. Munby, *The Idea of a Secular Society* (London, 1963), 14–32. Further citations to this work are given parenthetically in the text.

6. T. S. Eliot, *The Idea of a Christian Society* (London, 1939).

be homogeneous. . . . Homogeneity could in theory arise spontaneously,' but in reality conditions in modern societies are unlikely to bring this about, and 'a secular society is in practice a pluralist society, in so far as it is truly secular' (17). (c) 'A secular society is a tolerant society. It makes no attempt to enforce beliefs or to limit the expression of belief' (20). (d) 'Any society must have some common aims, in the sense that people are doing things together to produce certain effects.' But a 'liberal secular society, by contrast with most previous societies, does not set itself any overall aim, other than that of assisting as fully as possible the actual aims of its members, and making these as concordant with each other as possible' (23, 27).

Let us, for the moment, stand aside from Augustine and our central question, whether this is really the sort of society that the Augustinian political tradition encourages us to approve. Before I return to that, it will be helpful to summarise the main objections that have been raised against it in modern debate. I will therefore first sketch some of these; having looked at the principal objections I will then consider some of the ways in which they have been met. This, I am afraid, will be in large measure no more than going over well-trodden ground; but to answer the questions I have asked myself about the direction in which an *Augustinus redivivus* might point in our day, it is necessary groundwork.

Liberalism of the 'freedom plus groceries' variety has come under attack in recent decades from several directions. Most fundamentally, many philosophers have seen modern liberalism as the outcome of the failure of the 'Enlightenment project'. The best known and most distinguished protagonists of this type of critique have of course been Alasdair MacIntyre and Charles Taylor.[7] Arguments of this kind have been widely accepted and influential in modern ethical and political thought, especially, though not exclusively, among so-called 'communitarian' writers. They run, very roughly,

7. Of MacIntyre's work it is enough to refer here to *After Virtue* (London, 1981), *Whose Justice? What Rationality?* (London, 1988), and *Three Rival Versions of Moral Enquiry* (London, 1990). For Charles Taylor's work in this connection, see his 'Justice after Virtue', in *After MacIntyre: Critical Perspectives on the Work of Alasdair MacIntyre*, ed. John Horton and Susan Mendus (Cambridge, 1994), 16–43; to the essays gathered in his *Philosophy and the Human Sciences* (Cambridge, 1985), vol. 2; and to his lecture 'A Catholic Modernity?' in *A Catholic Modernity? Charles Taylor's Marianist Award Lecture*, ed. James L. Heft (New York, 1999), 13–37. John M. Rist, *Real Ethics: Reconsidering the Foundations of Morality* (Cambridge, 2002), also attacks such theories, though from a different point of view.

something like this: the scientific worldview of the late seventeenth and eighteenth centuries, generally adopted as the paradigmatic form of knowledge, led to a loss of a teleological vision of human nature and, with that loss, to the eclipse of virtue and the human good as the objectives of social living, permitting the emergence of individualistic theories that give the central place to freedom of choice. The result of the project is seen as moral emotivism and radical individualism.

The implication in the political sphere of the Enlightenment project is the overriding value ascribed to freedom and a need for neutrality on the part of the public authority. A modern liberal society is, by definition, based on the recognition, in the words of one of its most forceful advocates, the late Sir Isaiah Berlin, 'of the fact that human goals are many, not all of them commensurable, and in perpetual conflict with one another'.[8] Much of modern liberalism insists that public authorities must not discriminate between different goals and different visions of the good. Differential support for some particular view or views would be condemned as discrimination and ruled out in civil society.[9] Justice in a society so conceived would be purely procedural, retaining strict neutrality on substantive issues, that is to say on different views of the good and the ends of life. Such a community will assign supreme value to freedom of choice among goods, constructed by us to adopt as objects for our pursuit, leading to our individual satisfaction. This now widely popular mode of thinking, based on the priority of choice and freedom, often said to be characteristic of capitalist societies, excludes any reference to the good or to virtue. Moral, philosophical, and religious beliefs are held to belong to a private sphere beyond the scope of public interest.

8. Isaiah Berlin, 'Two Concepts of Liberty', in *Four Essays on Liberty* (Oxford, 1969), 171.

9. The case is well stated, and subjected to searching criticism, by Charles Taylor in 'Cross-Purposes: The Liberal-Communitarian Debate', in *Philosophical Arguments* (Cambridge, MA, 1995), 181–203. Cf. P. Pettit: 'Liberal/Communitarian: MacIntyre's Mesmeric Dichotomy', in Horton and Mendus, *After MacIntyre*, 178, quoting MacIntyre, *Whose Justice?* 335: 'The aspiration to provide a basis for political agreement between the adherents of different traditions and different conceptions of the good life, is maintained in the liberal way of thinking about politics. Sustained by liberal thought, the aspiration is influential in actual social and political affairs; it constitutes nothing less than "the project of modern liberal, individualist society"'.

Many theologians, philosophers, and political thinkers have come to repudiate such a project. The arguments are well enough known not to need spelling out here. It has been said that to state the conception, at any rate in its purest form, is enough to condemn it: 'The self-portrait of the individual constituted only by his wilfulness, liberated from all connection, without common values, binding ties, customs, values or traditions ... need only be evoked in order to be devalued.'[10] A society so conceived cannot transmit to its members a moral or cultural tradition in which they can learn how they ought to live and which could provide them with an identity; and any society based on such a principle would be too fragmented to be sustainable in practise. 'The moral universe projected by this form of liberalism appears to be a place in which self-interested individuals and groups engage in a continuous struggle for political power, while government stands above the battlefield, applies morally neutral procedural rules to adjudicate the conflicts.'[11] But to be human is to be situated in nature, a history, and a culture; it means to have a specific place in the world, in a tradition, and in a personal history shaped by and embedded in them which constitutes one's self. Among theologians, too, classical liberalism has found little support. Stanley Hauerwas, for instance, writes that 'liberalism, in its many forms and versions, presupposes that society can be organized without any narrative that is commonly held to be true;'[12] it cannot even provide a genuine freedom, which 'comes only by participation in a truthful polity capable of forming virtuous people'.[13]

Liberalism so understood has thus proved widely unacceptable, and many defenders of liberalism have restated it to make it less vulnerable to the kinds of criticism I have mentioned. I go on to summarise both the fur-

10. Michael Walzer, 'The Communitarian Critique of Liberalism', *Political Theory* 17 (1990): 8.

11. Ronald F. Thiemann, *Religion and Public Life: A Dilemma for Democracy* (Washington, DC, 1996), 97.

12. Stanley Hauerwas, *A Community of Character: Toward a Constructive Christian Social Ethic* (Notre Dame, IN, 1981), 12.

13. Hauerwas, *Community of Character*, 3. Cf. O'Donovan, *Desire of the Nations* (here aimed at 'classical republicanism'): Politics so conceived would be restricted to 'the defence of social structures which refuse the deeper and spiritual and cosmic aspirations of mankind', and pit 'political order against human fulfilment, [of] making the polis constitutionally hostile to philosophy, theology and artistic vision' (122; cf. also 244–46).

ther debate and what I take to be Augustine's position in relation to the issues raised by it under three headings.

The first point at which criticism has been directed is the underlying individualism. Margaret Thatcher put it bluntly in her famous dictum that there is no such thing as society. We need waste little time on this, for, as we have seen, it has been widely and convincingly rejected. Moreover, it is not really an issue at stake in our discussion of Augustine, for Augustine would certainly have agreed with modern critics in rejecting the unacceptable individualistic assumptions. Man, in his view, was created a social being; even the life of the saints is a social life. A fully human life and human fulfilment requires the society of our fellows. I do not need to dwell on this, as it has, so far as I know, not been questioned. Against this insistence on the essentially social nature of human life is to be set Augustine's strong stress on original sin. His approach to the nature of civic community is shaped by its overarching importance, at any rate from the time of the reorientation of his thought that took place in the mid-390s following his rereading of St Paul. The importance of this upheaval in his thought has been both exaggerated and played down;[14] but it would be hard to overestimate its importance in determining the overall shape of Augustine's thinking. Adam's sin became the foundation myth of the human condition. Paul had given Augustine a deepened sense of the power of sin in human affairs.[15]

A question mark came thus to hover over the link between the social world in which we live and act and the ultimate goal of human life. For Augustine, no social arrangements, no human justice or ingenuity, could establish the Kingdom of God or bring us any closer to it; only God's saving acts could do that. Social and political arrangements were the necessary medium

14. The literature is immense. For a recent (over-?) statement, see Kurt Flasch, *Logik des Schreckens. Augustinus von Hippo: De diversis quaestionibus ad Simplicianum I.2* (Mainz, 1990). The continuity of Augustine's thought on this theme has been emphasised, and the significance of this turning point in Augustine's intellectual career minimised, by Goulven Madec, *Introduction aux 'Révisions' et à la lecture des oeuvres de Saint Augustin* (Paris, 1999). For an extensive recent discussion, see Gaetano Lettieri, *L'altro Agostino: Ermeneutica e retorica della grazia dalla crisi alla metamorfosi del 'De doctrina christiana'* (Brescia, 2001). I would still maintain that reading Paul in the mid-390s changed the contours of Augustine's thought, although I would agree that some deep continuities in it have been obscured and need to be given adequate recognition.

15. The next two paragraphs summarise views I first worked out in Markus, *Saeculum*, and have repeated ad nauseam.

for the realisation of human objectives; what was natural to man, however, was subverted by sin. This is what has allowed the frequent misreading of Augustine which has emphasised its resemblance to contract-based theories of society at the expense of failing to recognise his insistence on the social character of human nature. The whole human order is fragmented, and community is fatally ruptured on every level: man is alienated from God, from his fellow men, and even from his own self. 'There is nothing' Augustine wrote in his old age, 'as social by nature and as antisocial [*discordiosum*] by corruption as the human race'; conflict within human societies is now more savage than among the fiercest of beasts.[16] The societies of fallen men are poised on the edge of chaos and perpetually liable to dissolution; all human effort has to be harnessed to the fostering of order. Justice, even at the minimal level attainable here, is hard to discern and to enact. Nevertheless the struggle to do so is a duty laid upon us: the demand is most movingly stated in Augustine's parable of the conscientious judge who is aware of the uncertainties of human justice and the inevitable frustration of his attempts to administer it. 'Will a wise man sit as a judge in this darkness of social living [*in his tenebris vitae socialis*], or will he not dare?' Augustine asks, and answers his own question: 'Of course he will sit; for this duty is laid upon him by the solidarity of human society on which he knows it would be wicked to turn his back.'[17]

Tension, conflict, insecurity are woven into the texture of human existence in its sinful state and draw narrow limits to the responsibilities and the efficacy of the public authorities. The agencies and institutions of society cannot serve to promote man's ultimate good; they serve only as means to turn human ferocity itself to the fostering of a precarious order, some basic cohesion which Augustine called 'the earthly peace'. In this 'hell on earth',[18] described in terms almost as sombre as Hobbes's state of nature, political authority and all the machinery of enforcement exist, as Augustine states it, *ut tuta sit inter inprobos innocentia:* to hold the wicked in check, to enable the virtuous to live untroubled among them. It can restrain wrongdoers by fear of punishment; it cannot aspire to make men good, though it can and

---

16. Augustine, *De civ. Dei* 12.28.1; cf. 23.
17. Augustine, *De civ. Dei* 19.6.
18. Augustine, *De civ. Dei* 22.22.4.

should secure a space for the free exercise of virtue by the virtuous and provide wrongdoers with the opportunity for amendment.[19]

For all that, Augustine could never conceive a fully human life except in a social context. In this respect his position is, *mutatis mutandis*, akin to that of modern critics of liberal individualism. If it is agreed that human living can be understood only within a social context, the second question that arises—both for modern critics of the liberal tradition and for Augustine—concerns the social implications of rejecting its individualism. What kind of society or group can or should embody the moral purposes that individuals should be taught and encouraged to pursue? The debate is over the question: At what level is this to be found, in what social grouping? At the level of the large-scale political community, the state—Augustine's *res publica*—or that of smaller communities, family, voluntary associations, groups of various kinds?

Critics of liberal individualism would be widely agreed on the central importance of the family, small groups, and voluntary associations, or more generally, of 'local forms of community within which civility and the intellectual and moral life can be sustained'[20] in shaping the moral life. One of these modern critics, Jeffrey Stout, took Augustine as his authority for the view of the political order that he advocates—an order

> that can secure private space in which we can form friendships and families and voluntary associations. In these spheres, not in the sphere of political doings, we find the closest thing to true happiness available in this life—analogues to the form of association the blessed enjoy in God's Kingdom. Politics at its best makes room for such happiness and such associations. It also opens up the space in which individuals can pursue the spiritual life as they understand it. Politics is no substitute for that

19. Augustine, *Ep.* 153.6.16. Cf. Augustine, *De Gen. ad litt.* 9.9.14: 'quantumque valeat ordo rei publicae in cuiusdam pacis terrenae vinculo coercens etiam peccatores'. Augustine's statement has a striking affinity not only with modern liberalism in the tradition of John Stuart Mill but also with the views of theologians who would allow the secular only a very limited value and restrict the function of secular power to that of 'protect[ing] the innocent and punish[ing] evildoers'. John Howard Yoder, *The Original Revolution: Essays on Christian Pacifism* (Scottdale, PA, 1971), 63, quoted and discussed by O'Donovan, *Desire of the Nations*, 151–52.

20. MacIntyre, *After Virtue*, 245.

and always goes sour the moment we begin thinking of an earthly political community, whether actual or potential, as our real home. . . . Liberal society is not the Kingdom of God. So, like all forms of political association in this life, it is radically imperfect. It is to be preferred not because it approximates the ideal but because its recognition of the limits of politics makes it not quite so bad as the other forms.[21]

I think Stout is partly right in claiming Augustine in support of a view of this sort: right in what he accepts, mistaken in what he rejects. So far as the family is concerned Augustine's position is also absolutely clear (and we can, for our purposes bypass other small groups, voluntary associations, and assume they would fall into the same category). The human family differs fundamentally from political society. The family, in Augustine's view, was founded in human nature. In this it contrasted radically with slavery, an institution brought about by the Fall. Political institutions were in their nature more like the latter than the former: that is, they belonged to man's fallen state.[22] The household, or extended family, is the community in which domination has no place; the hierarchy of command and obedience exists for the mutual good. Here rule is truly service, and obedience is learning or practising virtue. The political community, by contrast, belongs to fallen nature and is radically infected by sin. Political subjection will always be distorted by the play of power and domination. For Augustine the political community as a whole is on the face of it unlikely to qualify as a potential medium for teaching us how to live, and any bid it might make to do so should be suspect. But, as I shall try to show, this unlikeliness needs to be qualified.

To sum up this far: much recent debate has been concerned not so much with our first question—over individualism, against the claims of community—as with the second: questions about the nature and scale of the community in which moral value can be embodied, promoted, and taught. Augustine and many modern political thinkers would agree on the family

21. Jeffrey Stout, *Ethics after Babel: The Languages of Morals and Their Discontents* (Boston, 1988), 233–34. Stout does not cite Augustine directly, referring only to an article by Gilbert Meilaender, 'Individuals in Community: An Augustinian Vision', *Cresset*, November 1983, 5–10, which I have been unable to consult.

22. For Augustine on human nature as social, see, e.g., *De bono con.* 1.1; *De civ. Dei* 19.5; 3. For the comparison of family, slavery, and political subordination, see the discussion in Markus, *Saeculum,* 93–96 and 197–210. This has occasionally been called into question but is generally enough accepted to require no further defence here.

and small voluntary communities providing for this need; but they would differ on the question whether the political community—the state—has a part to play in meeting it.

This brings us to our third question, and this is where most disagreement arises. The debate we are concerned with—I want to avoid the labels of 'liberal' and 'communitarian' to characterise it—contrasts two views of the political community. According to one, 'The good life is pursued by individuals, sponsored by groups; the state presides over the pursuit and the sponsorship, but does not participate in either.'[23] According to the other, put forward by critics of the first view, what is required is 'a state that is, at least over some part of the terrain of sovereignty, deliberately non-neutral.'[24]

The opposition between the two alternatives has been very clearly stated by Alasdair MacIntyre:

> Where liberals have characteristically insisted that government within a nation-state should remain neutral between rival conceptions of the human good, contemporary communitarians have urged that such government should give expression to some shared vision of the human good, a vision defining some type of community. Where liberals have characteristically urged that it is in the activities of subordinate voluntary associations, such as those constituted by religious groups, that shared visions of the good should be articulated, communitarians have insisted that the nation itself through the institutions of the nation-state ought to be constituted to some significant degree as a community. . . . Communitarians have attacked liberals on one issue on which liberals have been consistently in the right.
>
> . . . [M]odern nation-states which masquerade as embodiments of community are always to be resisted.[25]

---

23. Walzer, 'Communitarian Critique', 16.

24. Walzer, 'Communitarian Critique', 16.

25. Alasdair MacIntyre, 'A Partial Response to My Critics', in Horton and Mendus, *After MacIntyre*, 302–3. MacIntyre makes a highly persuasive case for this view in his *Dependent Rational Animals: Why Human Beings Need the Virtues* (Chicago, 1999), 129–46. I am not entirely persuaded that 'the shared public goods of the modern nation-state are not the common goods of a nation-wide community and, when the nation-state masquerades as the guardian of such a common good, the outcome is bound to be either ludicrous or disastrous or both' (132).

Some liberal 'revisionists', as they have been called,[26] have argued, convincingly, in my view, for the need of 'some commonly recognized definition of the good life'.[27] The absolute opposition between a version of liberalism which upholds the requirement of strict neutrality, secularity, and pluralism by the public authority and a version in which 'a defense of pluralism need not involve the troubling concepts of governmental neutrality and secularity'[28] has softened in recent debate. Thus a distinction has been proposed between two versions of liberal theory by Michael Walzer (summarising the view of Charles Taylor):

> The first kind of liberalism ('Liberalism 1') is committed in the strongest possible way to individual rights and, almost as a deduction from this, to a rigorously neutral state, that is, a state without cultural or religious projects or, indeed, without any sort of collective goals beyond the personal freedom and the physical security, welfare, and safety of its citizens. The second kind of liberalism ('Liberalism 2') allows for a state committed to the survival and flourishing of a particular nation, culture, or religion, or of a (limited) set of nations, cultures, and religions—so long as the basic rights of citizens who have different commitments or no such commitments are protected.[29]

Walzer recognises that tension and conflict are inherent in this model of liberalism. Practical choices will be of a pragmatic kind, depending on the needs and character of the particular society, notably on the relationship between its minorities and the majority.

Charles Taylor, especially, has rejected liberal theories he characterised as 'procedural', which tend to assert that 'the principle of equality or nondiscrimination would be breached if society itself espoused one or other conception of the good life. This would amount to discrimination, because we

---

26. E.g., by Thiemann, *Religion and Public Life*, 105–14.
27. Taylor, 'Cross-Purposes', 182.
28. Thiemann, *Religion and Public Life*, 98.
29. See Michael Walzer, 'Comment' [on Charles Taylor's 'The Politics of Recognition' (1992)], and Charles Taylor, 'The Politics of Recognition', in Charles Taylor et al., *Multiculturalism: Examining the Politics of Recognition*, ed. Amy Gutmann (Princeton, NJ, 1994): 99–103 and 25–73, respectively. Walzer's quoted summary is from p. 99; cf. Taylor, "Politics of Recognition", 56–61.

must assume that in a modern pluralist society, there is a wide gamut of views about what makes a good life.'[30] As against such theories, he has maintained that 'functioning republics are like families in this crucial respect, that part of what binds people together is their common history. Family ties or old friendships are deep because of what we have been through together, and republics are bonded by time and climactic transitions.' Shared history and experience provide a society with an idea of its common good: 'the bond of solidarity with my compatriots in a functioning republic', as Taylor says, 'is based on a sense of shared fate, where the sharing itself is of value.' 'Patriotism involves more than converging moral principles; it is common allegiance to a particular historical community'; 'the good is what we share'.[31] Others have spoken of 'communities of character', described as 'historically stable, ongoing associations of men and women with some special commitment to one another and some special sense of their common life'.[32]

Could Augustine have accepted something like this? Even though the question posed in these terms could hardly have arisen for him, the place of moral value in the *res publica* did exercise him. We must, I think, concede that opposed tendencies in his thought were in tension, if not in conflict, here. On the one hand, he assigned great importance to a shared culture and shared values. On the other, his belief that sin has radically fragmented social life would incline him to be suspicious of claims on behalf of the political community's capacity to promote the moral life. Where we consider he might have come down on this question depends in large measure on the weight we give to one or other of these leitmotifs in Augustine's thought.

Let me start with the first, the importance of shared ends. I think that an *Augustinus redivivus* would be sympathetic to something like Walzer's 'Liberalism 2'. He clearly thought consensus, a shared culture and common purpose, so important that we have grounds for expecting him to have wanted

30. Taylor, 'Cross-Purposes,' 186.

31. Taylor, 'Cross-Purposes,' 192, 198, 190. Cf. Oliver O'Donovan's assertions in *Common Objects of Love* (Cambridge, 2002) that representative objects, persons, histories, ideas 'express what the society is, and what it is good for; they are forms of that knowledge of itself which is at the same time love of itself' (32) and that 'the claim of tradition is not the claim of the past over the present, but the claim of the present to that continuity with the past which enables common action to be conceived and executed' (33).

32. Michael Walzer, *Spheres of Justice: A Defense of Pluralism and Equality* (New York, 1983), 62, giving Otto Bauer's *Austro-Marxism* as the source of the phrase. The phrase was also used by Stanley Hauerwas as the title of his book, *Community of Character*.

to maximise these in his conception of society. For Augustine, the nexus of the objects of its members' 'cohesion of wills', or what Oliver O'Donovan has called its 'common objects of love', is what constitutes the society's value system, which defines it as this particular society and sustains it as such. We might, loosely, but in line with Augustine, think of it as its shared culture. In his treatise *De doctrina Christiana* he had classified elements within the secular culture in a scheme which distinguished the necessary, the useful, the admissible, and the inadmissible elements within it.[33] What was inadmissible was the religious content of a pagan culture: essentially, its idolatry (that, as a shared foundation, would form the basis of a demonic society).[34] Shared meanings and consensus on a value system are essential features of a society and form part of what the heavenly City recognises, sanctions, and fosters for its own ultimate purpose, the true worship of the one God. His *De doctrina Christiana* is deeply imbued with a sense of the crucial importance of a shared culture rooted in a shared tradition. The idea of a society without a shared moral basis, as little more than a mechanical agglomerate of separate juxtaposed groups each with its own goals, cuts across the grain of Augustine's thinking. Any institution or society is the bearer of a tradition of practise or practises; it embraces argument about the nature and content of its own tradition. A vital tradition has its own dynamism; both the dominant culture and the subcultures within it will undergo change over time, and the balance between them will be delicate and shifting, especially in the longer term. A living tradition has room for what Alasdair MacIntyre has called a 'continuity of conflict'; indeed, it is 'a historically extended, socially embodied, argument'.[35] Augustine's idea of the moral consensus on which a society rests could, I think, be benignly interpreted as embracing a dynamic consensus of this kind.

33. Augustine, *De doctr. Christ.* 2.19–25. Cf. above, chap. 2, pp. 38, 45.

34. I have explored this in Robert A. Markus, 'Augustine on Magic: A Neglected Semiotic Theory', *Revue des Études Augustiniennes* 40 (1994): 375–88; reprinted in Robert A. Markus, *Signs and Meanings: World and Text in Ancient Christianity* (Liverpool, 1996), 125–46. Idolatry might well be considered as a case of what Charles Taylor has described in 'A Catholic Modernity?' as a denial of transcendence: an 'exclusive humanism', 'based exclusively on a notion of human flourishing, which recognizes no valid aim beyond this' (19).

35. MacIntyre, *After Virtue,* 206–7.

In the *City of God* the point is made in somewhat different terms. Here the consensus at the roots of social existence is defined in more explicitly moral and political terms. Augustine leaves no possibility of doubting that the political community as such has moral objectives. As we have already seen in chapter 2, adopting Cicero's definition for his own purpose, Augustine was driven to the conclusion that the only true *res publica*, based on the only true justice, is the heavenly City. If we are to be able to speak of any other social grouping—from empires down to a band of robbers—as a *res publica*, we need a definition that does not include justice in the *definition* of the group. You will recall Augustine's famous story of Alexander and the pirate: when challenged about infesting the high seas, the pirate defended himself by telling the king that what he was doing differed from Alexander's empire only in scale: 'I do it with a little ship and am called a robber; you do it with a great fleet and are called an emperor'.[36] The point Augustine is making is not that societies are morally equally bad, or neutral, or all equally deficient, but that none can claim the only true justice, which is to be found only in the heavenly City.[37] They must necessarily fall short of that, but they can fall short in hugely differing degree. In relation to that all the values to which human groups are committed are relativised; but they are not invalidated. Any group or society is subject to moral evaluation: as Augustine neatly puts it, 'The better the objects which a society is agreed in loving,—the objects of its consensus, we might say—the better the society; the worse the objects, the worse the society'.[38] This is why Augustine proposes an alternative to Cicero's definition, one that is value-free, bracketing the requirement of justice, substituting for 'a multitude united in agreement about what is right',[39] the neutral formula 'united in agreement about what they love'.[40] Justice, or any other moral quality, is thereby removed from the definition of a political community. It has been said that Augustine has thus 'set up the standard of modern political thought against ancient, casting the political community off from its moorings in justice to drift on the tide of

36. Augustine, *De civ. Dei* 4.4.

37. And, indeed, they can be just even if they do not possess 'true' or 'perfect' justice: cf. chap. 2, n. 31.

38. Augustine, *De civ. Dei* 19.24.

39. 'Coetus iuris consensu et utilitatis communione sociatus'; Augustine, *De civ. Dei* 2.21.2; 19.21.1.

40. Augustine, *De civ. Dei* 19.24: 'rerum quas diligit concordi communione sociatus'.

popular consensus';[41] but it is important to recognise that though Augustine removes civil society from the sphere where perfect justice can be realised, he does not remove it from the realm where moral norms are applicable. They are yardsticks by which its quality is to be assessed, not part of its meaning.[42]

Augustine, I conclude, would certainly not have wanted to restrict the scope of the public realm to securing outward goods, order, security, and the means of living, and—like some modern liberal thinkers—he would have wanted to maximise the moral and cultural consensus which make it the society it is. And he would no doubt have extended the scope of the public realm to include as much as this consensus allowed. A *res publica* had to embody some moral qualities, and Augustine certainly expected its rulers to do their best to achieve this. But could such consensus include a shared religion?

Augustine, as we have seen, defined the ideally perfect society in eschatological terms. Being totally transcendent, it was thus removed from the range of anything that could be aspired to as a goal to be aimed at. Actual societies are too disrupted by sin and always at the mercy of the play of power, domination, and exploitation to get very far in the pursuit of the good. He was therefore anxious to limit the scope of the functions that can be expected of the political community. As Oliver O'Donovan put it recently, 'The most that one could reasonably expect of sinful and prideful communities was some consensus on goals worth pursuing'.[43] But though they cannot aspire to the peace and justice of the eschatological City, they can aim higher than the level of the den of robbers. How much higher?

There is no reason why a Christian (or Moslem, or Jewish) society, provided it was based on a genuine consensus and made no excessive claims for itself, could not be a 'sinful and prideful community'—as are all human societies—and yet express a 'consensus on goals worth pursuing' which might include some religious goals.[44] I think, however, that Augustine would have

41. O'Donovan, 'Augustine's City of God XIX', 96.

42. For further discussion, see 'Additional Note on Christianity in a Pluralist Society' in this chapter, pp. 66–69.

43. O'Donovan, *Common Objects of Love*, 21. Cf. Taylor, *Philosophy and the Human Sciences*: 'One of the most crucial dimensions of social life [is] . . . the degree to which the society constitutes a political community, that is, the kind and degree of shared ends' (2:99).

44. O'Donovan, *Common Objects of Love*, 21.

been reluctant to admit the possibility of a society more or less homogeneous in its religion, sharing a consensus on its ultimate purposes, and this for two reasons. The first is that it would run against the grain of his eschatologism: we should not expect the eschatological gap between Church and world ever to be closed, or come so close to being closed, in this world. A virtually wholly Christian society would be likely, in Augustine's eyes, to encourage a dangerous delusion about its distance from the eschatological City, to come perilously close to closing the 'eschatological gap' that must always yawn between it and any earthly city. The second reason is more practical: for the author of *City of God* the notion that religion could be among the shared ends of his society would have been inconceivable. Although he expected Christian emperors to place their power at the service of God 'by using it to spread its worship to the greatest possible extent',[45] he assumed that earthly societies would always contain conflicting views of the final good, as did the Roman Empire of his day.[46] As Augustine came to abandon, in the years after 400, his optimistic estimate of its comprehensive Christianisation, he came to see it in increasingly sombre tones. In his late work, especially in the *City of God,* Rome and the Christian community are even opposed, as 'they' and 'we', their representative heroes, writers, thinkers as 'theirs' and 'ours'. In his daily experience as a bishop, as we noted in the previous lecture, Augustine had to reckon with the inert weight of a pagan civic order.[47] His earthly City was inevitably what we would nowadays call 'pluralistic' in its nature, composed of diverse cultures, comprising groups dedicated, in Augustine's language, to love of different objects—that is, committed to different and conflicting value systems. Conflict over the ultimate purpose would be a permanent feature of society. A wholly Christian society was beyond any horizon that Augustine could have envisaged, and something he would have viewed with suspicion had he been able to do so.

This is, however, just what came into being in the Christian West in the course of a few centuries after him. And so vanished the possibility of defining the 'secular' as what can be shared by Christians with their non-Christian fellows. For several centuries the 'secular' came to be thought of as a separation of functions *within* a society defined in Christian terms. The medieval Church never quite lost a sense of having to resist being fully

45. Augustine, *De civ. Dei* 5.24.
46. See chap. 2.
47. See chap. 2.

embedded in the society around it; it needed to keep some critical distance. But a sense of the autonomy of the secular was destroyed, at any rate until a new pluralism in Western Europe brought it back into the realm of historical reality from the sixteenth century on. This will form the subject of my last chapter.

Additional Note on Christianity in a Pluralist Society

Reconciling approval of a society which reflects all our beliefs and our value system with acknowledging the liberty of others to reject our beliefs and values must begin with affirming that we are free and equal moral persons, with our own moral claims, and entitled to respect for our different moral commitments. This is presumably part of the meaning of the Christian conception of love, with the obligation it imposes to respect the integrity of others. 'Christian love that respects the freedom of others to exercise their moral capacities surely includes the freedom of Christians to live within and support a system of justice which does not enforce patterns [of distribution] that favour distinctively Christian ends.'[48]

Augustine excluded religion from the scope of the consensus required by the heavenly City during its earthly pilgrimage; but he would have rejected

48. H. R. Beckley, 'A Christian Affirmation of Rawls's Idea of Justice as Fairness', pts. 1 and 2, *Journal of Religious Ethics* 13 (1986): 210–41 and 14 (1988): 229–46; for the quote, see 14 (1988): 237. At this point, we must take note in parentheses of a serious problem that arises in this connection which will no doubt have been gnawing at the back of many readers' minds, concerning Augustine's 'paternalistic' readiness to approve coercive love. I only signal it here in passing; discussion of it would take me too far afield. It is clear that his endorsement of the coercion of heretics and schismatics runs counter to his views on the functions of the civil community. It is, however, the implications of an Augustinian type of view on the latter that I am considering here; if I were trying to give a complete account of Augustine's views on religious coercion as well as of the civil community—a task too large to undertake and not to the point here—I would probably have to acknowledge a tension between his views on coercion and on the functions of the civil community, a tension which may indeed prove to be irresolvable. (I have discussed this problem in Markus, *Saeculum,* but am still uncertain about it.) We should, however, note that Augustine advocated coercion only within the Christian community (including schismatic bodies), not in the civil community at large. This, by implication, confirms the relative independence that the latter would have in his view.

the absolute disjunction between what John Rawls calls a 'general and comprehensive' conception of justice and a 'political conception' which 'tries to elaborate a reasonable conception for the basic structure [of society] alone and involves, so far as possible, no wider commitment to any other doctrine.'[49] I think that in terms of this vocabulary Augustine would assert a link of some sort between the two. He would see Rawls's 'basic structure' as a minimum condition of social coherence, but as a minimum that societies above the level of the band of pirates would generally manage to improve on. The best they can manage must, however, fall short of the ideal, if for no other reason than because it can embrace only as much of a value system as can be generally shared by members of the civil community. Its Christian members will, of course, be further committed beyond this restricted sphere to the pursuit of other, more ultimate, objectives and will also seek to bring the goods comprised within the 'political justice' of the earthly peace into some sort of alignment with their ultimate objectives. The extent to which this will be possible in political practise must depend on the range of Rawls's 'overlapping consensus of reasonable comprehensive doctrines'[50] current within the particular society. 'The freedom to agree to a public conception of justice does not prevent Christians (or others) from advocating their beliefs and accompanying way of life to other persons, individually or collectively, as long as they do not attempt to enforce that way of life through the basic structure of society.'[51]

What Augustine shares with political thinkers who embrace some such version of 'overlapping consensus' is the view that there is a shared area of social ethics which binds people together in a nation-community, while leaving them free to adhere to their own various beliefs. As Charles Taylor remarks, 'This political ethic will typically not exhaust the common identity by which people are bound together. This will include some particularistic elements—of history, language, culture, even in some cases, religion'.[52] This implies, as does Augustine's view of human societies as composed of the two Cities overlapping in the *saeculum*, that people will have different reasons

---

49. John Rawls, *Political Liberalism* (New York, 1996), 13; cf. 134.

50. Rawls, *Political Liberalism*, 134.

51. Beckley, 'Christian Affirmation', 235.

52. Charles Taylor, 'Modes of Secularism', in *Secularism and Its Critics*, ed. Rajeev Bhargava (New Delhi, 1998).

for accepting the shared social ethic.[53] The convergence is embedded in diverging fundamental (or 'comprehensive') belief systems and moral assumptions. In a living, healthy society, argument over these will continue, within the framework of a shared tradition, without jeopardising common allegiance to shared principles.

In any society that is not virtually homogeneously Christian, there is bound to be a gap between a Christian view of human social existence—as indeed any other view with a religious or metaphysical basis—and the overlapping consensus. To ignore this gap is to make unreasonable claims on a mixed society: claims such as I considered in my second chapter, which in effect amount to a rejection of the 'secular'. An illuminating example of such a position is furnished by Oliver O'Donovan. O'Donovan rejects a 'proposal [by Jacques Maritain] for a "democratic secular faith", which the Church is to advocate in common with non-Christians in public, while each, in the semi-privacy of its own educational establishments, gives different reasons for it (*Man and state*, ch. 5). What that means is that the democratic "creed", not the Gospel, becomes the heart of the Church's message to the state'.[54] To this we must reply: no, it does not mean that. It means quite simply that the Church proclaims its message of salvation to all but that it also feels morally bound to uphold the consensus on which civilised public order is built. To endorse a shared loyalty which falls short of a Christian's loyalty to the gospel is not a betrayal and does not imply thinking of society in amoral, quasi-mechanical, terms as being driven purely by 'internal dynamics rather than led by moral purposes'.[55] It is to deny only the kind of claims commonly made by upholders of the ideal of 'Christendom', implicitly affirming a Christian duty to seek to shape society and political forms.

53. Cf. *De civ. Dei* 18.54: members of the two Cities make use of the same finite goods, although for different ends, with 'a different faith, a different hope, a different love'. Cf. John Rawls, 'Justice as Fairness: Political Not Metaphysical', *Philosophy and Public Affairs* 14 (1985): 223–51: in overlapping consensus 'each of the comprehensive philosophical, religious, and moral doctrines accepts justice as fairness in its own way; that is, each comprehensive doctrine, from within its own point of view, is led to accept the public reasons of justice specified by justice as fairness . . . as theorems, as it were, at which their several views coincide. . . . The doctrines in an overlapping consensus differ in how far they maintain a further foundation is necessary and on what that further foundation should be' (247–48). For fuller discussion, see his *Political Liberalism*, 11–15 and 190–95.

54. O'Donovan, *Desire of the Nations*, 219.

55. Cf. O'Donovan's account of society considered as a 'secular' reality in *Desire of the Nations*, 246–47; quotation from 246; for his critique of neoliberal views, see 211–12.

O'Donovan, however, goes on to restate his view of the Church in relation to the society around it. This restatement is offered as a further description but in fact specifies a radically different conception, and one that is not open to the objection of being 'triumphalist', of seeking a position of influence for the Church. In this formulation the Church is less concerned to shape or influence the society around it than to deliver its message to it: 'Christian political order is [not] a *project* of the church's mission, either as an end in itself or as a means to the further missionary end. The church's one project is to witness to the Kingdom of God. Christendom is a *response* to mission, and as such a sign that God has blessed it. It is constituted not by the church's seizing alien power; but by alien power's being attentive to the church.'[56]

This model asserts no claim to religious influence over the public realm; in fact, it repudiates the exercise of religious power in civil society. The power of the gospel is to be mediated through continuing public debate, without threatening the autonomy of the secular order. This is an important alternative to the generally proposed idea of Christendom as the Church's project to subjugate rulers to the yoke of Christ. Indeed, it reflects much more faithfully the permanent duality of Church and world in the present *aiôn,* the 'eschatological gap' between proclamation and hearing.[57] Theologians such as Karl Barth or John Howard Yoder, to whom any convergence between Church and state is suspect, have warned us against blinding ourselves to anything that could appear to close this gap. Their protests are a salutary warning. But Augustine's eschatologism and the theology of the secular based on it achieve the same end without forcing us to surrender the value of our 'common objects of love'.

---

56. O'Donovan, *Desire of the Nations,* 195 (italics in original). Cf. pp. 213–14 for O'Donovan's view on Barth.

57. See chap. 1.

4

FROM AUGUSTINE TO CHRISTENDOM

I must begin this last chapter with a brief backward glance. In my first chapter I sketched how Christians gradually came to accept more and more of the secular realities of the Roman world—what Peter Brown somewhere called the 'technology of Mediterranean living'—and, especially from the time of Constantine onward, to make it their own, absorbing it into the stuff of their Christian existence and moulding it to their purposes. After Constantine the Christian takeover of Roman civilisation gained momentum. The Eusebian vision of Roman Empire and Christian Church providentially fused in a single, universal, Christian society was becoming a reality. Within a century of Constantine's conversion to Christianity, being a 'Roman' had come to be much the same as being a 'Christian'. Of course, an old-fashioned, secular Roman identity could be tenaciously maintained for some decades; but this was largely confined to literary elites clinging to traditional forms. More typical among Christians would be the sort of view articulated by the historian Orosius. In the year 417 Orosius, a Christian native of Roman Spain who had fled to North Africa, could write: 'When I, a refugee from trouble and upheaval, flee to a haven of security, I find everywhere my native land, everywhere my law and my religion. . . . As a Christian and as a Roman, it is to Romans and Christians I come.'[1] Against this merging of Christian and Roman identities, Augustine's voice was a cry of

---

1. Orosius, *Adv. pag.* 5.2.

protest. In chapters 2 and 3 I showed that in his reflection on human living in history and in society, he sought to safeguard a space for the secular, for the swaths of human life—the Roman 'technologies of living'—which, in a right understanding of Christianity, have an autonomy that should be preserved.

Others had shared Augustine's disquiet about the almost total assimilation of Roman culture, lifestyles, and values and feared a consequent undermining of a distinctive Christian identity. Though sharing such anxieties, they turned in a different, indeed opposed, direction to deal with them. Thus Pelagius and his followers sought to impose the exacting standards of the ascetic on the Church as a whole.[2] They wanted to ensure that the Church would, in Harnack's words that I quoted in chapter 1, '[stand] out . . . in bold relief'[3] in the society around it. They were puritan reformers who wanted the line which divided full-blooded, authentic Christianity from mediocrity to become the boundary of a reformed Christianity. Beyond it there was to be only the unregenerate world of paganism; for mediocrity there was to be no room. Augustine had wanted to give *Lebensraum* to Christian mediocrity, to assure the Roman *homme moyen sensuel* of his rightful place in the Christian congregation.

I shall not defend this view of Augustine's theology, having done so at tedious length elsewhere.[4] Both Augustine's defence of Christian mediocrity and Pelagian disapproval were opposed to any class distinction in the Church between the ordinary workaday Christian and the seeker after perfection. For Pelagius, the division was overcome in the universality of the call to perfection; for Augustine, in the universality of the need for grace. All are

2. On this, see above all the studies of Peter Brown: 'Pelagius and His Supporters: Aims and Environment', in *Journal of Theological Studies*, n.s., 19 (1968): 93–114; 'The Patrons of Pelagius: The Roman Aristocracy between East and West', in *Journal of Theological Studies*, n.s., 21 (1970): 56–72; and, for the background, 'Aspects of the Christianisation of the Roman Aristocracy', *Journal of Roman Studies* 51 (1961): 1–11, all three reprinted in his *Religion and Society in the Age of Saint Augustine* (London, 1972). For general surveys of the *status quaestionis*, see Gerald Bonner, *Augustine and Modern Research on Pelagianism* (Villanova, PA, 1972; reprinted in his *God's Decree and Man's Destiny*, Collected Studies [London, 1987]; and F. G. Nuvolone, 'Pélage et Pélagianisme', in *Dictionnaire de la spiritualité* 12 (1986): 2889–2942.

3. Adolf von Harnack, *The Expansion of Christianity in the First Three Centuries*, ed. and trans. James Moffat (London, 1904), 1:349.

4. Robert A. Markus, *The End of Ancient Christianity* (Cambridge, 1990), esp. chaps. 4 and 5. I here summarise my comparison of Augustine and Pelagius on 64–66.

called to pursue perfection; none attain it here, but all are commanded to run so as to obtain the prize (1 Cor. 9:24; Philipp. 3:12). Perfection was the distant goal. But this is where the ways part between puritan impatience with imperfection and Augustinian impatience with puritan perfectionism. For Augustine imperfection is inescapably woven into man's fallen condition, and grace is the only gateway to salvation. In the last resort, within the Christian community Augustine could admit only one division, that between those destined to be saved and the reprobate; and this was hidden in the mysterious depth of God's will, not to be revealed before the end.[5] In this life on earth what mattered was incorporation into the community of the redeemed by baptism and a continuing life of prayer, love, humility, and repentance.

The clue to Augustine's distinctive view of the secular is his persistent eschatologism. That is what allowed him to give space to areas of subtler shades between the puritan reformers' ruthless dichotomy of black and white. In contrast, Augustine located the secular in the *saeculum,* in that intermediate and temporary realm in which human affairs unfold before the end. 'Sacred' and 'profane' were too starkly final as categories, too 'ultimate', too closely tied up with salvation and damnation, to describe our temporal affairs. Or, as Gerard Manley Hopkins depicted our condition in his great and truly Augustinian poem 'Spelt from Sybil's Leaves':

> Lét life, wáned,
> ah lét life wind
> Off hér once skéined véined variety upon, áll on twó
> spools; párt, pen, páck
> Now her áll in twó flocks, twó folds—black, white; right
> wrong...

but not until the day is ending and 'our night is over us and will whelm us'. Until then, Augustine insists on protecting what Hopkins would have called the 'dapple' of our moral existence. If I may be allowed to change poets in midstream:

---

5. Augustine, *De civ. Dei* 15.1.1. On this theme, see Robert A. Markus, *Saeculum: History and Society in the Theology of Saint Augustine,* 2nd ed. (Cambridge, 1988), passim, and chap. 2. For Henri-Irénée Marrou's comment insisting on the need for an eschatological understanding of Augustine's view, see chap. 2, n. 10.

... the enchainment of past and future
Woven in the weakness of the changing body,
Protects mankind from heaven and damnation.
    —T. S. Eliot, *Burnt Norton*

But Augustine's trichotomy did not last. It was eclipsed by simpler, but morally harsher, dichotomies, not unlike the demands made by Pelagius and his followers. The chief of the agencies that brought about this erosion of the middle ground was the pervasive influence of the ascetic movement. Ascetics did not insist, as had Pelagius and his followers, on their severe standards being imposed on all. But the prestige that asceticism acquired in Western Europe, through the power exercised by bishops and clergy often trained in monastic communities and dedicated to an ascetic spirituality, extended the sway of its standards far beyond the circles of its active practitioners.[6]

The ascetic model set up a simple polarity between Christian perfection and, over against it, worldliness, the secular, the profane, all amalgamated in a single category: the world, the flesh, and the devil, as later Christian language would say. The norm was, in principle, attainable, or at least, approachable, if only by a few, or, as the fifth-century ascetic Salvian insisted, 'a very few'. This elitism was impatient with the run-of-the-mill religion of the mass of ordinary Christians. A central theme in the polemic common to Pelagius, to ascetic writers such as Salvian and Caesarius of Arles, and to many later Christian writers was the opposition between baptised Christians, Christians 'in name only', and real, authentic Christians, dedicated to the pursuit of Christian perfection. The Christian community was to conform itself to the ideal of the Apostolic Church as depicted in the Acts of the Apostles. The image of the primitive Christian community in Acts 2 and 4 was used not only as a charter for communal monasticism but also as a myth of reform for the Church at large. It was not the few but the Christian people as a whole that was held to be then 'so perfect'.[7] And now the whole

---

6. This is the argument of a large part of Markus, *End of Ancient Christianity*. On the whole theme, see the sensitive exploration by Conrad Leyser, *Authority and Asceticism from Augustine to Gregory the Great* (Oxford, 2000).

7. Salvian, *Ad eccl.* 3.10.41–43 (cf. Markus, *End of Ancient Christianity*, 169–77). I have treated this topic in R. A. Markus, 'Church Reform and Society in Late Antiquity', *Reforming the Church before Modernity: Patterns, Problems, and Approaches*, ed. Christopher M. Bellito and Louis I. Hamilton (Aldershot & Burlington, VT, 2005), 3–20. For the use of

Christian community was to be, as it was then, of one heart and mind in God and to hold all things in common. The apostolic community was as much a permanent challenge to the lukewarm Church of the present, which had betrayed the purity of its origins, as it was a model for the segregated, monastic, communities. The pattern admired and striven for was a Christian community that 'stood out in bold relief' from the secular world around it, a sect in the world of unregenerate mediocrity merged with the world of paganism and idolatry. Use and enjoyment by Christians of the secular world, accepted as a fact of life, were elided.

The opposition between these two models is, in the abstract, clear enough; in fact, of course, historically they were interwoven in Christian thought and living. The decisive period in which the balance was shifting towards the ascetic pole was the first three decades of the fifth century: the time of the old Augustine. Augustine and his fellow bishops saw the problem of Christianisation in terms of a struggle of Christianity against the inert weight of an ancient, unconverted world. They ceased, slowly, to see the Christianisation of the Empire as a 'stunning, supernatural victory'[8] over the pagan gods. The ever-present weight of the pagan past called for a redirection of effort. Christianity would need, not to struggle for sudden victory, but to fight a slow, grinding guerrilla war against ancient custom, with no victory in sight.

For it was not just a question of outward allegiance: the bishops were constantly alert to traces of the unregenerate past, and they were ready to diagnose its presence in daily practises that seemed innocuous to most people: anniversary banquets, the shows and races in circus and theatre, the celebration of the New Year, dancing, processions, the performance of traditional gestures to honour the emperor's image, and so forth. The festivals of the Roman calendar, observed by Christians unproblematically in the mid–fourth century, were growing suspect and by the end of the fifth century were in large measure eliminated from the Christian calendar. Examples of the boundaries of Christianity being more rigidly drawn could be multiplied.

---

the Acts image, see A. de Vogüé, 'Monachisme et Église dans la pensée de Cassien', in *Théologie de la vie monastique,* Théologie 49 (Lyon, 1961), 213–40, who distinguishes two versions of the myth, one of which points to secession from the pagan world, the other to secession both from that and from the Church.

8. Peter Brown, *Authority and the Sacred* (Cambridge, 1995), 26.

The spectrum of what was tolerable within traditional Christian observance was contracting. We can watch the process in Augustine's day, for example, in the residual observances of the imperial cult, just on the point of vanishing: 'Why do you [Christians] venerate such pictures with a public gesture of *adoratio*; why do you render such honour to men while you claim to be giving it only to God? you, for whom adoring images, whether painted on wax or engraved on metal, is abomination? . . . Why don't your priests [*sacerdotes*] prohibit this?' So the pagan interlocutor asks his Christian mentor in a dialogue probably contemporary with Augustine's growing disenchantment with the Christianisation of the Theodosian Empire. The embarrassed Christian answers that although it is certainly forbidden to adore anything in heaven or on earth, habit prevents people from being weaned from their erroneous ways. But, he adds, what is rejected is 'ill-advised homage, not worship rendered to divinity [*incautum obsequium non diuinum cultum*]. . . . And although stricter Christians [*districtiores Christiani*] abhor this custom of such heedless deference and the clergy keep forbidding it', it nevertheless does not amount to idolatry.[9] Such anxieties were new. The range of what is allowable was under pressure from the *districtiores Christiani*; and clerical authority was being mobilised to enforce the more rigorous ascetic norms. Much that had been previously unquestioned was becoming demonised, or, to use the language of this book, being pushed from the realm of the secular into that of the profane. The boundaries were shifting, their locus depending on the balance between the tenacity of established custom and clerical authority.[10]

The latter could be deployed in a variety of ways. In 406 Paulinus of Nola, for instance, as Dennis Trout has shown in a perceptive study, 'was willing to create and promote a sanctioned Christian context for the enactment and reshaping of certain rituals rooted in the pre-Christian traditions

---

9. *Consultationes Zacchaei et Apollonii* 1.28, ed. J. L. Feiertag, *Questions d'un païen à un chrétien*, Sources chrétiennes 401, 402 (Paris, 1994), and now the excellent study by M. A. Claussen, 'Pagan Rebellion and Christian Apologetics in Fourth Century Rome: The *Consultationes Zacchaei et Apollonii*', *Journal of Ecclesiastical History* 46 (1995): 589–614. Feiertag favours the first decade of the century and suggests 408–10 (16–22); Claussen, the early 390s. Feiertag, *Questions*, 86, observes that so far as this kind of practise was concerned, there was no 'véritable mise en question' before about 430. Cf. his summary on *adoratio*, 68–75, and his discussion of the debate on the imperial cult, 80–93. The legal prohibition of the practise dates from 425 (*CTh* 10.4.1).

10. On this theme, see Robert A. Markus, 'L'autorité épiscopale et la définition de la chrétienté', *Studia Ephemeridis Augustinianum* 58 (1997): 37–43.

of the Italian countryside'.[11] Creative reinterpretation of this kind, however, was rare before Gregory the Great's time. More often bishops were becoming less inclined to adopt the more easygoing tolerance of earlier times. Augustine had long ago acknowledged that the Catholic Church numbered among its members some who indulged in questionable practises, such as venerating pictures, from superstition, from their passions, or from oblivion concerning their duty to God. He refused to condone these dubious habits but excused them as something to be expected 'in so great a multitude of people'.[12] Writing some fifteen years later, he again conceded that there were many bad Christians just as there were many bad pagans, addicted to all sorts of questionable habits. But at least, unlike the pagans who allowed such things to happen undenounced, Christians had priests in the Church who prohibited them. The horizons were closing in.

It was, however, not only the ascetic impulse and its growing prestige and influence that brought about the narrowing of the range of Christian culture in the century and a half after Augustine's death. The ascendancy of ascetic ideals was accompanied by a transformation in Western European societies. The impoverishment suffered by their culture between Augustine and Gregory the Great amplified the effect of the pressure of ascetic attitudes. In Augustine's world—as we have seen again and again—much of the ancient intellectual, ritual, and cultural tradition was still too alive to be written off. It was a society which still contained a rich fabric of intellectual and religious traditions of great diversity. Membership within the Christian community through baptism was the only clear difference to define a Christian among his fellows; all else, except idolatry, could be shared.

This changed drastically in the decades following Augustine's death and even more in the following century.[13] For Gregory the Great, at the end of the sixth century, the very question would have seemed redundant, for, as he

---

11. Dennis Trout, 'Christianizing the Nolan Countryside: Animal Sacrifice at the Tomb of St Felix', *Journal of Early Christian Studies* 3 (1995): 281–98.

12. Augustine, *De mor. eccl.* 34.75; cf. Augustine, *C. Faust.* 20.21, and comment by John Kevin Coyle, *Augustine's 'De moribus ecclesiae catholicae': A Study of the Work, Its Composition and Its Sources,* Paradosis 25 (Fribourg, 1978), 419–24.

13. The substance of this paragraph is taken from Robert A. Markus, *Gregory the Great and His World,* 40–41. I also approached this topic in Robert A. Markus, 'The Sacred and the Secular: From Augustine to Gregory the Great', *Journal of Theological Studies,* n.s., 36 (1985): 84–96; reprinted in Robert A. Markus, *Sacred and Secular: Studies on Augustine and Latin Christianity* (London, 1994), and in *Augustine,* vol. 2, ed. John M. Dunn and Ian Harris, Great Political Thinkers 3 (Cheltenham, 1997).

was fond of saying, in this time of easy conformity, now that the age of persecutions was over and the Church was at peace, everyone was a Christian.
There might still be some who did not carry the Christian name; but if there
were such, they were marginal, and Gregory was more interested in those
who did bear the name but were like the *iniqui* who 'deviate from righteous-
ness by the wickedness of their works', who were Christians in name only,
from outward conformity.[14] The excluded few—marginal groups like Jews,
heretics, rustics labelled by bishops as pagans—were characterised in religious categories, measured by norms laid down by Christian clergy.[15] His
was a radically Christian world—what we have become accustomed to
call 'Christendom'—and Gregory was comfortable in it in a way Augustine
could never have imagined.[16] Gregory's world was the result of some two
hundred years of cultural development since Augustine's time, and we must
consider this, however briefly, before considering its end-product, the society in which 'everyone was a Christian'.

It was something of the sort that Henri-Irénée Marrou, the greatest historian of Late Antiquity, had in mind when he spoke of the emergence after
the end of antiquity of a society wholly sacral *(sacrale)*:

> Since the whole edifice of the culture [*civilisation*] of antiquity, not just
> its educational institutions, was in danger of collapse, it was the Church
> itself that had to assume, to take charge of the culture, its instruments, its
> means of action, substituting itself for the failing empire. This is the
> source of what was to become one of the most distinctive characteristics
> of the Western Middle Ages: the society it animated was a 'sacral Chris-
> tendom', to make use of a phrase so usefully applied by Jacques Maritain.
> It appears to us as organised around a single pole, that of religion, in-
> deed, I would go further and say, of the Church. [17]

---

14. Gregory, *Mor.* 18.6.12.

15. Gregory, *Hom. in Ev.* 2.32.5; 1.11.3; cf. Gregory, *Hom. in Hiez.* 1.10.37; 2.3.14, and in-
numerable texts in which Gregory writes about Christians 'in name only'.

16. Cf. John M. Rist, *Augustine: Ancient Thought Baptized* (Cambridge, 1994), 290,
291.

17. Henri-Irénée Marrou, 'La place du Haut Moyen Age dans l'histoire du christian-
isme', in Centro italiano di studi sull'alto Medioevo, ed., *Il passaggio dall'Antichità al
Medio Evo in Occidente,* Settimane di Studio 9 (Spoleto, 1962), 595–630, 608.

The culture of the Latin Middle Ages was the end-product of a development which began in Late Antiquity. It differed from *la culture augustinienne*, even though 'both were of religious, of Christian inspiration'.[18] Marrou himself, famously, made Augustine's *De doctrina Christiana* the foundation charter for a culture subordinating all forms of intellectual activity to a scriptural faith and making them serve its purposes. In the late Roman world of Augustine, however, 'there was a cultural ideal shared by pagans and Christians, an ideal realised in a manner often analogous to the materials and techniques of expression borrowed from classical tradition'.[19] To this culture that conformed to Augustine's formula, without the severance from its classical roots, Marrou gave the name 'theopolis', which he described as 'a religious culture, a Christian culture, as rigorously subordinated to a religious ideal as the culture of the Latin Middle Ages, but without breaking, as that did break, the continuity of its link with the classical origins from which it derived'.[20] The possibility of such a cultural symbiosis slowly vanished from Western society during its transformation in the two centuries after Augustine. The collapse *(l'effondrement)* of a set of institutions and of a culture which had in Late Antiquity, even in its Christianised form, kept its 'autonomy' brought about the conditions for this 'sacral' society.

It is important to stress the gulf between Augustine, according to Marrou the originator of this cultural recipe, and those who followed its prescriptions, of whom Marrou cites Julianus Pomerius, Caesarius of Arles, and Gregory the Great as examples: 'In their culture one observes the human impoverishment [*l'appauvrissement humain*] to which Augustinianism, more and more narrowly interpreted, has brought them'.[21] This *appauvrissement* marks a decisive break between Augustine and the epigoni. For Augustine, though an upholder of the culture of the 'theopolis', was himself a

18. Henri-Irénée Marrou, *Saint Augustin et la fin de la culture antique* (Paris, 1938; reprinted with his *Retractio,* 1949), 608 (page citation to 1949 edition).

19. Marrou, *Saint Augustin,* 691–92.

20. Marrou, *Saint Augustin,* 695.

21. Marrou, *Saint Augustin,* 684. Mark Vessey, in his editorial introduction to part 4 of *The Limits of Ancient Christianity: Essays on Late Antique Thought and Culture in Honor of R. A. Markus* (Ann Arbor, MI, 1999), 210, notes that 'Marrou it was who, having once essayed a liberal Catholic apology for a proto-medieval Augustine similar to the one portrayed by Harnack, later reverted to a view more like Troeltsch's, in which the bishop of Hippo stood for a relatively short-lived, post-Constantinian "culture of the Theopolis," common to Christians and non-Christians alike'.

product of, and we might say, still inhabited, the Hellenistic-Roman culture of what Marrou called the *paideia*: the cosmopolitan and pluralistic culture of the highly mixed and sophisticated urban society of Augustine's North Africa. This background was shared to a steadily diminishing extent by Augustine's successors.

This sea-change was, obviously, the work of several centuries, and this is not the occasion to trace its stages in any detail. The watershed, it seems reasonably clear now, was the second half of the sixth century. It is difficult not to have a sense of a huge shift that separates the mental world inhabited by Boethius, Cassiodorus, and their contemporaries—say, the first three decades of the century—from that inhabited by Gregory the Great at its end. I suspect that this shift is obvious to any reader of their works. But it is easier to be aware of it than to describe it—not because it is too subtle but, on the contrary, because it is too enormous, too all-embracing.

We should remind ourselves at the outset that when Cassiodorus died (around 580) in his nineties Gregory was around forty. The two worlds overlapped. In the course of his long life Cassiodorus had experienced the process we are trying to diagnose and gave us hints of his awareness of a new world—one he called the 'modern' world, apparently being the first to use the word 'modern' in this way[22]—which he saw emerging from the ruins of the world he had known. Cassiodorus, the descendant of at least three previous generations of aristocrats, all distinguished in public service, held, following in their footsteps, a variety of offices under the Ostrogothic regime, culminating in the praetorian prefecture of Italy. He had devoted all his working life to promoting the partnership of Goth and Roman within what he called one *civilitas*. When this broke down under the impact of the Byzantine reconquest, his position became impossible and he retired from public office. This was in the late 530s. He had already shown a deep interest in a Christian religious culture. Probably in 535–36 he had formed a plan with Pope Agapitus to found an institute of advanced Christian studies in Rome.[23] Apart from what this tells us about the direction that Cassiodorus's

22. James J. O'Donnell, *Cassiodorus* (Berkeley, CA, 1979), 235, referring to Walter Freund, *Modernus und andere Zeitbegriffe des Mittelalters* (Cologne, 1957), 27–40.

23. Cassiodorus, *Inst., Praef.* 1. The reference to *cum beatissimo Agapito papa urbis Romae*, though not conclusive, suggests that the plan was made during Agapitus's pontificate (535–36). Cf. also O'Donnell, *Cassiodorus*, 196. On the project and its fate, see Henri-Irénée Marrou, 'Autour de la bibliothèque du pape Agapit', *Mélanges d'Archéologie et d'Histoire de l'Ecole Française de Rome* 48 (1937): 124–69.

own interests were taking, his account is highly instructive as to the state of affairs in Rome. What he wanted to do, he explained, was to match the flourishing state of secular studies by providing resources to have Christian professors paid to teach publicly in Rome.

Before we follow Cassiodorus's career further, it is worth pausing over his testimony to the vigour of secular studies in Rome. There is no reason to doubt the opening words of his *Institutes*—'I was aware of the enthusiasm for the study of secular letters'. There is no reason to doubt his words; they echo a very similar statement made not long before him by the African theologian Facundus,[24] whose works were in Cassiodorus's library; and there is a fair amount of scattered evidence to confirm them. Sicilian aristocrats were still in the habit of sending their sons to be educated in Rome, teachers were still underpaid,[25] and around the middle of the century Gregory the Great could still receive an education by no means negligible in Rome, as could Venantius Fortunatus in Ravenna.[26] Roman crowds gathered for four days running in the year 544 to hear Arator declaim his epic on the Acts of the Apostles. The classics were still being copied by leisured aristocrats;[27] learned theological treatises, among them Facundus's, were read by lay people, and lay men—and women!—had well-stocked libraries, which could assist scholars and facilitated what nowadays some would call their 'networking'. There were still foci of learned enterprise even outside the walls of the cloister. Examples could be multiplied;[28] they reveal a level of activity which was certainly not extensive and might not be high but was not negligible. 'Much of the writing of the period', in the judgement of one of its most careful recent investigators, 'leaves an impression of earnest endeavour.'[29] Even the austere work of Boethius found an audience, restricted

24. Facundus of Hermiane, *Pro def.* 12.4.12.

25. Cassiodorus, *Var.* 9.21.

26. For a survey, see Pierre Riché, *Éducation et culture dans l'Occident barbare, 6ᵉ–8ᵉ siècle*, 2nd ed. (Paris, 1962), 96–139; see also O'Donnell, *Cassiodorus*, 180–82.

27. Cf. L. D. Reynolds and N. G. Wilson, *Scribes and Scholars: A Guide to the Transmission of Greek and Latin Literature*, 3rd ed. (Oxford, 1991), 39–43.

28. Riché, *Éducation et culture*, 119–26.

29. See especially S. J. B. Barnish, 'Maximian, Cassiodorus, Boethius, Theodahad: Literature, Philosophy and Politics in Ostrogothic Italy', *Nottingham Medieval Studies* 34 (1990): 16–32; quote on 32. He also remarks here that 'authors could sometimes play amongst their serious activities'. I am grateful to Dr. Barnish for generous advice concerning these paragraphs.

though it may have been to his circle of friends.[30] Neither this nor the philosophical sophistication of the *Consolation of Philosophy* or his other writings would have been conceivable fifty years later.

When Boethius composed his commentary on Aristotle's *Categories*, in 510, the year of his consulship, he already had a sense of foreboding about the future. The chores of his office, he wrote, had distracted him from his main duty, the task of educating the Roman public;[31] he was afraid that the liberal arts were threatened by neglect.[32] He could not have foreseen the calamities that were to bring about something far worse than the sad state of things he apprehended. Within ten years of his death at the hands of the Gothic regime, Justinian launched the wars of reconquest. Almost continuous warfare, mopping-up operations in the North still continuing in the 560s, and within three years of Justinian's death (in 565) the new invasion of the Lombards were only the beginning of Italy's afflictions. Despite the pretence of a return to normality announced in the *Pragmatica Sanctio* of 554, few Italians can have enjoyed the 'former happiness' which Narses, Justinian's victorious general, was credited with having brought back to Italy.[33] From 542, plague repeatedly swept through Italy, as through the other provinces of the Empire. Its first and most virulent outbreak is estimated to have carried away as much as a third of the population in the affected areas.[34] What concerns us here are the permanent consequences rather than the temporary crises, spiritual and material. War and plague certainly contributed heavily to the social, demographic, and economic changes that transformed Italian society in the second half of the sixth century. The flight

30. H. Chadwick, introduction to *Boethius: His Life, Thought and Influence*, ed. Margaret Gibson (Oxford, 1981), 1–12. Chadwick notes his sense of isolation: 'It is a small circle, and the treatises on logic did not make him new friends. They contain a large number of unhappy references to contemporary critics who were altogether failing to see any value in his labours on Aristotle' (2).

31. Boethius, *In cat. Arist.* 201.

32. 'Multumque ego ipse iam metuo ne hoc [neglectus] verissime de omnibus studiis liberalibus dicatur'. Boethius, *In cat. Arist.* 230C.

33. *Auc. Hav. ext.*, 3: 'totiusque Italiae populos expulsis Gothis ad pristinum reducit gaudium'.

34. For a summary, see P. Allen, 'The "Justinianic" Plague', *Byzantion* 49 (1979): 5–20. There is now an excellent study of the questions and controversies concerning it: Peregrine Horden, 'Mediterranean Plague in the Age of Justinian', in *The Cambridge Companion to the Age of Justinian*, ed. Michael Maas (Cambridge, 2005), 134–60.

of the aristocracy, the collapse of the traditional forms of civil government, and the emergence of more localised societies dominated by military and clerical elites have been well and fully described.[35] The classes on whom the continuity of learning and culture depended were, in effect, fragmented, if not wiped out.

Cassiodorus was among the few who, having taken refuge in Constantinople, returned to Italy in the 550s. His life had already taken a new direction in the late 530s, when he retired from public office. He published the *Variae,* his collection of official correspondence during the Gothic regime he had served faithfully for thirty years. Along with it he published a religious treatise: *De anima.*[36] It was the other leaf of the diptych: he wrote it, he says, 'not in obedience to the command of kings', but in a profound inner dialogue with himself.[37] Heavily indebted to Augustine, especially to the *De quantitate animae,* it is far more overtly religious than Augustine's philosophical treatise. Cassiodorus is more at home in Jerusalem than in Athens: he contrasts the *magistri saecularium litterarum* with the authority of 'true doctors' *(veracium doctorum . . . auctoritas)*—the evangelists;[38] throughout the work, religious rather than philosophical argument is preponderant.[39] The work closes with a meditation on the Last Things and a prayer, full of echoes of Augustine's *Confessions.* Like this last, the *De anima* marks a conversion.

Not, of course, the conversion of a non-Christian to Christianity; but that of an aristocrat and civil servant to the life of a *vir religiosus.*[40] He himself referred to this new direction his life was taking as a *conversio,* although not until much later.[41] It seems possible that Cassiodorus had formed a plan

35. T. S. Brown, *Gentlemen and Officers: Imperial Administration and Aristocratic Power in Byzantine Italy, 554–800* (Rome, 1984).

36. Cassiodorus, *Variae* 11, *Praef.* 7. On the link between the two, see O'Donnell, *Cassiodorus,* 114.

37. Cassiodorus, *De an.* 2.

38. Cassiodorus, *De an.* 4.

39. As a single illustration I cite the proof in *De an.* 4 (lines 127–37) of the soul's immortality, for which Cassiodorus offers man's being made in the image and likeness of God (Gen. 1:26) as the knockdown proof.

40. As Pope Vigilius referred to Cassiodorus in his *Ep. ad Rust. et Seb.* (*PL* 69.49 A/B). On Cassiodorus's conversion, see O'Donnell, *Cassiodorus,* 107–14.

41. Cassiodorus, *De orth.* (1240C): 'post Commenta Psalterii ubi, praestante Domino, conversionis meae tempore primum studium laboris impendi.' This suggests that Cassiodorus thought of his 'conversion' as dating to soon after the *De anima,* in the early 540s.

to found the Vivarium, his monastery in Calabria, before his departure to Constantinople;[42] but he took up permanent residence there only on his return, laden, it seems, with books acquired in Constantinople. His old plan for a Christian centre of learning and his monastic enterprise now coalesced. Its fruit was the *Institutes of Divine and Human Learning* and the monastic community for which it was intended as its rule. Perhaps some twenty years later, in his ninety-third year, he wrote a little treatise on writing correctly, addressed to his monks, apparently at their request. In this he returned to one of the themes that the *Institutes* had touched on. That Cassiodorus's last work was a treatise on correctness in writing addressed to his monks should not allow us to underestimate either his achievement or theirs. Cassiodorus, as recent studies have established, 'had inspired or fostered a particular interest both in religious studies, and in the secular disciplines'; and his community 'continued to serve with intelligence similar interests in the world outside, perhaps as late as the papacy of Gregory the Great.'[43]

For all that, Cassiodorus knew he was writing his last work, the treatise *On Correct Writing* for a world much changed since the days of his Gothic masters. What his monks needed was not the education he had shared with Boethius, Ennodius, Maximian, and their generation. Their needs were for more immediate access to the 'essential reading' helpful in understanding the Scriptures and the basic techniques of understanding and exposition.[44] Like Boethius and Cassiodorus in their day, the monks of the Vivarium were to be an elite in their world; but it was a very modest intellectual culture that was to make them so. The options of the 530s were no longer available in the 580s.

Cassiodorus, then, is the living link between two eras: the first decades of the sixth century, in which a lively literary culture and circles in which it was valued could still be taken for granted, and the final decades of the century, when these conditions of a flourishing secular culture had in large measure

42. On the foundation, O'Donnell, *Cassiodorus*, 189–92.

43. S. J. B. Barnish, 'The Work of Cassiodorus after His Conversion', *Latomus* 48 (1989): 157–87. Quotations are from 186. On the *Institutes* and Cassiodorus's work as a whole, see now also the magisterial introduction by Mark Vessey to *Cassiodorus: Institutions of Divine and Secular Learning; On the Soul*, trans. James W. Halporn (Liverpool, 2004), 1–101.

44. Cassiodorus, *De orth.* (1270B). I have borrowed the content of this paragraph from Markus, *End of Ancient Christianity*, 219–20.

disappeared.[45] He is also, in his own person, an emblem of the changed nature of the intellectual culture that did survive into the new world. We have noted the growing religious focus of his work. Like Augustine, Cassiodorus subordinated the secular disciplines to scriptural studies and placed them entirely within their framework. But, of course, it had been one thing to insist on this around AD 400 and quite another to do so around 580. Augustine, as Marrou remarked, had no interest in the institutional aspects of a Christian culture; unlike Cassiodorus, he proposed a syllabus, not a school. He could take for granted the institutions which would furnish educated Christians with the instruments which would enable them to form a Christian culture.[46] Augustine wrote at a time of a thriving city-life, which furnished the conditions for lively intellectual interchange; the liberal arts were indeed still apt to be claimed as the distinctive mark and the rightful property of a pagan elite. It was one thing to assert a claim to a stake in them on behalf of Christians, as Augustine did in his *De doctrina Christiana*, and something quite different to encourage—as did Cassiodorus in the project of the *Institutes*—a Christian elite to enrich their constricted intellectual life and to keep its horizons as wide as circumstances, and the library at the Vivarium,[47] would permit.

The conditions Cassiodorus had known in his youth had largely vanished from Gregory the Great's Italy—and, *a fortiori*, from the rest of Western Europe—for good. Although, as I have said, he had received an education in Rome which by any standards must rank as respectable, there is no evidence that such an education could still be had at the end of the sixth century. Gregory liked to describe his own work as a despicable little trickle compared with the deep torrents and the clear flow of Augustine and Ambrose.[48] He was, indeed, well read in the Latin Fathers; Augustine and Cassian made a deep mark on his thought. But compared with theirs, his intellectual world was hugely simplified. At the simplest level, Augustine's work,

---

45. For a fascinating sidelight on this change, see now Mark Vessey, 'From *Cursus* to *Ductus*: Figures of Writing in Western Late Antiquity: Augustine, Jerome, Cassiodorus, Bede', in: *European Literary Careers: The Author from Antiquity to the Renaissance*, ed. Patrick Cheney and Frederick A. de Armas (Toronto, 2002), 47–103.

46. Marrou, *Saint Augustin*, 400–401.

47. The index of R. A. B. Mynors's edition of the *Institutes* should warn us not to overestimate its resources, especially in the range of classical authors it contained.

48. Gregory, *Hom. in Hiez. Praef.*; Cf. Gregory, *Ep.* 10.16. Compare Cassiodorus's preface to his *Exp. Psalm.* (lines 10 ff.).

and that of his contemporaries, presupposed an active and lively debate among contemporaries who did not always share the same religion or the same worldviews. Even in the time of Cassiodorus, real, educated paganism was still in the air and could at times flare into real life.[49] Cassiodorus could speak of rich, noble, and powerful pagans being daily converted to the true religion through the Lord's mercy; and he thought such converts were often 'like Saul the persecutor after his conversion' among the Christian intellectual elite.[50] For Gregory, pagans of this kind, on one's doorstep, with whom one might engage intellectually, were unimaginable. His pagans were rural backwoodsmen to be coerced into decent Christian living and worship by their betters; and even when he had to imagine more distant pagans beyond the boundaries of the known world, it was on this model he had to construct them. Paganism of the distant past appears, for instance in the *Dialogues,* through a haze of folklore.[51] On no terms could pagans enter into current debate or contribute to a culture. Classical thought and literature are quite simply absent from Gregory's works, or they reached him filtered through the patristic literature that he knew. In contrast with Cassiodorus, Gregory was a man of one book. His world was bounded by the horizons of the Christian Scriptures and could be readily deciphered in their terms. Christianity had become unquestionable and had come to define the contours of discourse.

The Church had come to swallow up the world. In an earlier age the great divide would have run between the Christian community and the unregenerate world outside it; for Gregory it ran—now that everyone was a Christian[52]—between the less and the more perfect within the Church. The complex heterogeneity of Augustine's world had collapsed into the more homogeneous simplicity of Gregory's. He could think of *conversio* more easily as something undergone by the Christian soul on its way to perfection than as the conversion of a non-Christian to Christianity.[53]

---

49. Procopius, *GW* 25.18 ff.

50. Cassiodorus, *Exp. in Psalm.* 103.16 and 13. My attention was drawn to these passages by Dr. S. J. B. Barnish.

51. On Gregory's pagans, see Robert A. Markus, 'Gregory the Great's Pagans', in *Belief and Culture in the Middle Ages,* ed. Richard Gameson and Henrietta Leyser (Oxford, 2001), 23–34.

52. Cf. above, pp. 77–78.

53. Gregory, *Hom. in Hiez.* 1.10.9–11. See also Carole Straw, *Gregory the Great: Perfection in Imperfection* (Berkeley, CA, 1988), 194–235, and Claude Dagens, *Saint Grégoire le Grand: Culture et expérience chrétiennes* (Paris, 1977), 247–346.

I have suggested elsewhere[54] that at the heart of this shift in the moral *imaginaire* lies a new relation between a text—that of the Bible—and the interpretative community for which it is the authoritative text. Gregory could read his world *through* the Bible with an ease Augustine could not have dreamed of. The significations of the text that Augustine had to struggle to recover, for whose validation he felt driven to identify rules, gave Gregory little or no trouble. He could see straight through them—or rather past them—to the world of the Spirit and could then return to the letter, enlightened by the Spirit. New habits of ascetic reading—not only texts, but pictures, indeed the visible and tangible world—made them more translucent; like a dead metaphor which has lost its original reference, the solidity and opacity of the world, like the 'presence' of the image, had dissolved along with that of the letter of the Bible. The meaning revealed was now closer, more accessible, than the revealing symbol. We are dealing here with a huge change in Christian sensibility, which Peter Brown has described as 'a watershed in the Christian imagination that falls somewhere in the late sixth century'.[55]

It need hardly be said that this hiatus in the culture of Late Antiquity is peculiar to the Latin West. It would be impossible to write anything corresponding to Glen Bowersock's account of a non-Christian Hellenism,[56] or rather some Latin analogue of it, continuing in the West. To be sure, there were some parallels. Averil Cameron, among others, has drawn attention to decisive changes, specifically to changes centred on the life of texts, images, and symbols in communities, in the Christian culture of the Byzantine world at much the same time. The realignment involved 'the replacement of the existing vestiges of classical culture by a codification of knowledge based on religious truth'.[57] In the epilogue of her Sather Lectures she spoke of a

54. I have discussed more fully the implications of this in Robert A. Markus, *Signs and Meanings*, chaps. 1–2.

55. Peter Brown, 'Images as a Substitute for Writing', in *East and West: Modes of Communication*, ed. Evangelos Chrysos and Ian Wood (Leiden, 1999), 32. He also remarks that 'it was precisely this sharp sense of "otherworldliness" that had been gloriously absent in large areas of the late antique Christian mentality' (30–31). In his book *The Rise of Western Christendom*, 2nd ed. (Oxford, 2003), he makes the point more widely, locating 'a profound change in the imagination' in the period 550–650 (220).

56. Glen W. Bowersock, *Hellenism in Late Antiquity* (Cambridge, 1990).

57. Averil Cameron, 'The Language of Images: The Rise of Icons and Christian Representation', in *The Church and the Arts*, ed. Diana Wood, Studies in Church History 28 (Oxford, 1992), 1–42; quotation from 33.

'closing in of intellectual horizons' taking place in the Eastern Empire in these years around AD 600.[58] In the West, intellectual horizons closed in very differently; all the same, there are important analogies between the ways that Christian discourse in the end emerged, in Averil Cameron's words, as 'a liberating as well as a totalizing influence' in the East as well as in the West.[59]

Nevertheless, the hiatus that had come to divide Augustine's world from Gregory's has no real parallel in the Greek East. No single writer could furnish a better illustration of this hiatus than Isidore of Seville. When Isidore set about the task of reassembling a cultural heritage for his age, he was not drawing from a current cultural repertoire but assembling 'collectibles' of earlier ages. The philosophical content of his *Etymologies* has been aptly characterised as 'une poussière d'extraits'; his work 'shatters the structures of ancient thought by reducing the intellectual apprehension of the world to the fragmented vision of the grammarian and the scholiast'.[60] Isidore's achievement was to lay the foundations for a new start, and by that very fact it demonstrates the depth of the hiatus between the past and the future.[61]

Theopolis was being superseded by Christendom—by a religious culture rigorously subordinated to a religious ideal, but now involving a break in the continuity of its link with the classical origins from which it derived[62]—even before Christianity assumed a new role in the Germanic societies that were becoming consolidated in formerly Western Roman provinces. Throughout its history within the Roman world, Christianity had been in the main re-

---

58. Averil Cameron, *Christianity and the Rhetoric of Empire* (Berkeley, CA, 1991), 228–29. Here she redefines the old problem of Christian culture in terms of the power of discourse in shaping and expressing social relationships. Christian rhetoric was moving 'into the central areas of political discourse'. On the same theme, see also her 'Images of Authority: Elites and Icons in Sixth-Century Byzantium', *Past and Present* 84 (1979): 3–35, and 'Byzantium and the Past in the Seventh Century: The Search for Redefinition', in *Le septième siècle: Changements et continuités/The Seventh Century: Change and Continuity*, ed. Jacques Fontaine and J. N. Hillgarth, Studies of the Warburg Institute 42 (London, 1992), 250–71.

59. Cameron, *Christianity*, 229.

60. Jacques Fontaine, *Isidore de Séville et la culture classique dans l'Espagne Wisigothique* (Paris, 1959), 676, 829.

61. This crude statement is intended to summarise the conclusion of Fontaine's great study, esp. 807–30.

62. The allusion is to Marrou's distinction between his 'theopolis' and the Christian culture of the Latin Middle Ages in *Saint Augustin*, 695. See p. 79 above.

ceptive, appropriating a cultural legacy and inheriting ready-made institutions which had matured over a long period. It had learned to live within a culture which it had little part in creating. Now in the new societies of Western Europe the Church was called to be creative rather than receptive. It readily assumed the role of a teacher, imposing its own mature traditions, in large part shaped by its Roman legacy, on the developing Germanic nations.

A central thread of these lectures has been the danger to Christianity of becoming too closely identified with the social structure and culture of its social matrix. If it had been constantly exposed to this risk since the Constantinian revolution, it became unable to avoid it in the course of the collapse of Roman culture and institutions and the emergence of Germanic Western Europe. Its social matrix was becoming one that the Church had shaped, and continued to shape, for itself.

Its dominant role in shaping Western Christendom was, however, purchased at a price that historians sometimes fail to reckon with. Until recently it was possible to think of Christendom as the zenith of Europe's historical destiny, the European *telos*. For a Roman Catholic historian such as Christopher Dawson, it was the source of European identity, which had to be recovered if Europe was to fulfil its historical destiny.[63] Only the most incurable Christian romanticism would now see matters in this way. Of course, we should not underrate the extent of the legacy of classical culture and institutions transmitted to Europe by the Church and the very creditable part played by churchmen in imposing Christian standards, more often than not Roman in their origin, on deeply rooted Germanic practises. Nor is it appropriate to disparage, in the name of attacking all 'triumphalism', the Church's part in moulding Western societies and a common European culture and to fail to acknowledge the mainly Christian sources of European civilisation.

But, equally, it would be irresponsible not to count the cost.[64] Western Christendom was enabled to close in on itself. Its estrangement from the Eastern churches was compounded by the loss of North Africa to Islam. The see of Rome was left without rival in Western Europe. Consolidating its authority over Western Christendom from the eleventh century, it no longer had, in its isolation, anything to learn, was no longer exposed to the fruitful

---

63. On this aspect of Dawson's work, see most recently Richard H. Roberts, *Religion, Theology and the Human Sciences* (Cambridge, 2002), 226–28.

64. This is the theme of Markus, 'Church Reform.'

tensions which had in the ancient Church secured some give-and-take between major centres of ecclesiastical authority, each with its own tradition. The Roman see assumed near-absolute authority over an increasingly consolidated hierarchical Church, as did that Church over the secular world around it. In becoming the unchallenged mistress of Western Europe, the Church became dangerously identified with a culture and a social order more constricting than ever, for it now inhabited a more homogeneous world largely of its own making. As the Church's domination extended, what I have called the 'eschatological gap' between Christ's lordship and the world to which it was being proclaimed was closing dangerously.[65] A twelfth-century historian could see the Christendom of his day as the final growing together of the heavenly and the earthly Cities—so much so, he wrote, that since Constantine and especially since Theodosius, 'it seems to me that I have been writing the history not of two Cities, but, almost, of one, which I call "Christendom" [*ecclesia*]'.[66]

Within the scope of this book I have to ride roughshod over the moments of Western European history when Christendom has been challenged in one way or another: the Reformation, the Wars of Religion, the Enlightenment, and the nineteenth century with the variety of doubts it raised. In our days, there is no general agreement about Christendom. What some theologians have called 'Constantinianism' is, at bottom, obliviousness to the crucial gap between the Church and the world, and 'Christendom' is the name under which the state of affairs corresponding to it has generally come to be designated.[67] Whether seen in political or cultural terms or in

---

65. On this, see chap. 1, pp. 14–15.

66. Otto of Freising, *Chron.* 5, *Praef.* It was in the circle of his uncle, Frederick Barbarossa, that the phrase 'Holy Roman Empire' originated.

67. On the different ways of understanding the idea, see Alan Kreider, 'Introduction', in *The Origins of Christendom in the West*, ed. Alan Kreider (Edinburgh, 2001), viii. He refers to O'Donovan's conception of the idea without quoting fully his definition: 'I use the term "Christendom" (in keeping with a good deal of current discussion) to refer to a historical idea: the idea of a professedly Christian secular political order, and the history of that idea in practice. Christendom is an *era*, an era in which the truth of Christianity was taken to be a truth of secular politics' (*Desire of the Nations*, 195). Kreider contrasts this with that of John Van Engen, 'The Christian Middle Ages as a Historiographical Problem', *American Historical Review* 91 (1986): 519–52: an all-embracing Christian society which, 'rooted in practice and profession and given shape by liturgical, ecclesiastical and credal structures, included every person in medieval Europe except the Jews' (546).

terms of the geographical extension of the defining features which are held to have constituted it, its passing is variously lamented or welcomed but never doubted. Thus a distinguished American theologian, Stanley Hauerwas, entitled a series of lectures *After Christendom?* What he wished to reject was the 'Constantinian set of presumptions that the church should determine a world in which it is safe'.[68] I have argued in these lectures that this rejection could claim to be well anchored in a Christian tradition championed, supremely, by Augustine.

It is fitting to conclude with a tribute to Pope John XXIII, in whose honour these lectures have been instituted. For it was he, together with the council he called and over which his genius presided, if somewhat fitfully, that reversed sixteen and a half centuries in which the spell of Constantinianism, or if you prefer, of Christendom, held the Catholic Church in its thrall.[69] Pope John had the courage and the vision to put an end to the Church's aspiration to determine a world in which it could be safe. On the contrary: it was no longer to be comfortable in the world but to be open to it, to learn from its ways, to engage in unending dialogue, sharing all that is truly human, the joys, hopes, fears, and anxieties of this age.[70] With the Blessed Pope John XXIII the Church has come to embrace the secular and to acknowledge its value, its autonomy, and even, if I may add what may seem paradoxical, its sacredness or holiness.[71]

---

68. Stanley Hauerwas, *After Christendom? How the Church Is to Behave if Freedom, Justice, and a Christian Nation Are Bad Ideas* (Nashville, TN, 1991), 18. However, it is to be noted that Emmanuel Mounier published his *Feu la Chrétienté* in 1950!

69. I would agree with Karl Rahner's view that one of two of the great revolutions in the Church's history is the mid-twentieth-century 'opening' to the world. That, in his view, brought to an end the middle period in the Church's three ages. (His first caesura, however, was not, as I would want to say, the Constantinian age, but the Church's opening to the Gentiles at Antioch.) See Karl Rahner, 'Basic Theological Interpretation of the Council', *Theological Investigations* 20 (1981): 77–89. Cf. also his essay 'The Abiding Significance of the Second Vatican Council', *Theological Investigations* 20 (1981): 90–102.

70. See Pope John XXIII, *Gaudium et spes*, §§ 1, and, for instance, 40, 44, 92.

71. See Introduction, n. 27.

INDEX

Gregory the Great (*cont.*)
    vs. Augustine, 87, 88
    and the Bible, 87
    Dialogues, 86
Grotius, Hugo, 7

Harnack, Adolf von, 79n.21
    on Christians as third race (*tertium genus*), 17–18, 72
Hauerwas, Stanley, 2n.3, 8
    After Christendom?, 91
    Community of Character, 61
    on liberalism, 54, 54n.13
heresy, 23, 33, 66n., 78
histories, ecclesiastical, 32, 33
Hobbes, Thomas, 56
Hollerich, M. J., 44n.33, 51n.4
homogeneity, religious, 6–8, 64–65, 86
Hopkins, Gerard Manley: 'Spelt from Sybil's Leaves,' 73
human nature, 51, 53
    Augustine on, 56–57, 58
Huntington, Samuel, 4

identity, Christian, 17–18, 22–28, 24n.33, 32–33, 71–72
individualism, 53, 54, 55–57, 60
Inglebert, Hervé, 27n.
Isidore of Seville, 88
Islam, 89

Jesus Christ
    as Incarnation, 14, 35, 36
    kingship of, 14–15, 28–30, 35, 90
    new age in, 14, 17, 25, 28–30, 35
    parousia of, 14, 35, 36
Jews and Judaism, 15n.6, 17–18, 19, 21, 78, 90n.67
John XXIII, 11–12, 91
John Paul II, 11n.27

Julian, 38
justice
    Augustine on, 42–44, 56, 63–64, 63n.37
    in liberalism, 7n.20, 53, 67, 68n.53
    Rawls on, 7n.20, 67, 68n.53
Justinian, 82

Kingdom of God, 35, 69
    Paul on, 14–15, 28
    relationship to human society, 10, 14–17, 28–30, 55, 57–58
Kreider, Alan, 26n.40, 90n.67

Lactantius, 19, 19n.21
Lakeland, Paul, 13n., 43n.28
Lepelley, Claude, 34n.7
Lerner, Max, 51n.4
Lettieri, Gaetano, 47n., 55n.14
Leyser, Conrad, 74n.6
liberalism
    and Augustine, 10, 41, 45, 49, 51, 55, 57–58, 57n.19, 64, 66–67
    consensus in, 51–52, 53, 68n.53
    criticisms of, 54–61
    defined, 10n.
    freedom of choice in, 53
    individualism in, 53, 54, 55–57, 60
    justice in, 7n.20, 53, 67, 68n.53
    neutrality in, 51–52, 53, 54, 54n.13, 59–61
    relationship to capitalism, 53
    the state in, 53, 57, 57n.19, 59–60
Licinius, 22
Lizzi, Rita, 34n.7
Lombards, 82
love
    of God, 16, 38, 43, 44, 47
    of neighbor, 43, 44, 66
    of self, 46, 47

Sentences of Sextus, 25
Severus, Septimius, 20
Song, Robert
 Christianity and Liberal Society, 2n.3,
  8n., 10n.
 on liberalism, 10n.
Sotinel, Claire, 12, 34n.7
state, the. *See* political authority and
 institutions
Stout, Jeffrey, 57–58, 58n.21
Straw, Carole, 86n.53

Taylor, Charles, 38, 67
 on idolatry, 62n.34
 on liberalism, 52, 53n.9, 60–61
 on secularism, 7
Tellenbach, Gerd, 16n.11
Tertullian, 18, 19, 20
Thatcher, Margaret, 55
Thélamon, Françoise, 37n.13
Theodosius I, 10, 21, 34, 37, 76, 90
 Cunctos populos, 31–32
Thiemann, Ronald F., 54n.11
tolerance, 10, 20–21, 52, 66, 77
Tornau, C., 43n.31
triumphalism, Christian, 30, 31–34, 33n.,
 36, 37, 39
 defined, 9
Troeltsch, Ernst, 79n.21
 on the sect-type, 30
Trout, Dennis, 76–77

United States vs. Western Europe, 1–2, 7

Van Engen, John, 90n.67
Van Oort, Johannes, 51n.4
Vatican Council, second, 11, 91

Vessey, Mark, 79n.21, 85n.45
Vogüé, A. de, 74n.7
voluntary associations, small, 57–59
Volusianus, 39, 39n.19

Walzer, Michael, 54n.10, 59nn.23, 24, 60,
 61–62
Wars of Religion, 7, 8, 90
Weigel, George, 4
 on Constantinianism, 11n.27
Western Europe
 Berger on, 4
 vs. Eastern Europe, 11n.26, 87–88
 Middle Ages in, 4, 11, 26, 65–66,
  78–79, 90n.67
 secularisation in, 1–2, 4
 in 6th century, 8, 11, 28, 80, 84–85,
  87–88
 vs. United States, 1–2, 7
 See also Christendom
Williams, D. H., 23n.
Williams, Rowan, 26n.43, 42n.27, 51n.4
Wilson, Bryan, 2, 30n.

Yoder, John Howard
 on Augustine, 25n.37
 on the Church, 24–26, 26n.43, 69
 on Constantinianism, 8, 24–26,
  25n.37, 26n.42
 The Original Revolution, 16, 26n.41,
  57n.19
 on political authority and institutions, 16n.12, 17, 26, 26nn.41, 43,
  57n.19, 69
 The Politics of Jesus, 16, 26nn.41, 43
 The Priestly Kingdom, 30n.
 on the state in the New Testament,
  16n.12, 17

ROBERT A. MARKUS

is professor emeritus at the University of Nottingham. He is the author of several books, including *Saeculum: History and Society in the Theology of St. Augustine*, *The End of Ancient Christianity*, and *Gregory the Great and His World*.